T0360985

For my parents, TQ

For Dexter and Tracie, MBG

Chinese Foreign Direct Investment

A subnational perspective on location

TAO QU
The University of Hong Kong

MILFORD B. GREEN
The University of Western Ontario

Routledge
Taylor & Francis Group

LONDON AND NEW YORK

First published 1997 by Ashgate Publishing

Reissued 2018 by Routledge
2 Park Square, Milton Park, Abingdon, Oxon, OX14 4RN
711 Third Avenue, New York, NY 10017

Routledge is an imprint of the Taylor & Francis Group, an informa business

Publisher's Note
The publisher has gone to great lengths to ensure the quality of this reprint but points out that some imperfections in the original copies may be apparent.

Disclaimer
The publisher has made every effort to trace copyright holders and welcomes correspondence from those they have been unable to contact.

A Library of Congress record exists under LC control number: 97070886

ISBN 13: 978-1-138-61793-3 (hbk)
ISBN 13: 978-0-429-46143-9 (ebk)

Contents

Figures and tables

Preface

Milford B. Green
Tao Qu

December, 1996

Interest in the spatial aspects of foreign direct investment has surfaced as one of the newer areas of research. Both in economics and business studies, space is being recognized as an important component in the foreign direct investment decision process. This somewhat late recognition of space is not surprising. As economic geographers have long known, space is a difficult concept to understand and analyse. As a colleague has observed, there seems to be a one way conduit between economic geography and its sister disciplines, economics and business. Economic geographers assimilate findings from those disciplines but geographic research results seldom seem to flow back. This is unfortunate for all concerned. Indeed surprise is often expressed that economic geographers conduct such research. Hopefully this book will help provide a linkage.

This book deals with the role of space and its economic children: relative location, distance and the urban hierarchy. All of these play a role in the distribution of investment dollars in a foreign country. This is because economic opportunity, risk and information availability are all conditioned by space. Every investment decision has a spatial component, whether it is explicitly recognized or not.

The People's Republic of China is a good choice for the examination of the effect of geography on foreign direct investment. It has only recently attracted large inflows of capital that are being affected by spatially explicit development policies. China thus provides an opportunity to study the effect of such policies as well as the effect of geography on foreign direct investment flows. This examination of subnational foreign direct investment flows is one of the features of this book that sets it apart.

The other feature is the construction of an explicitly spatial framework for the study of foreign direct investment. Economic geography can provide (and already has) substantial contributions to the study of foreign direct investment This book is the latest in a series of steps toward understanding how geography affects foreign direct investment.

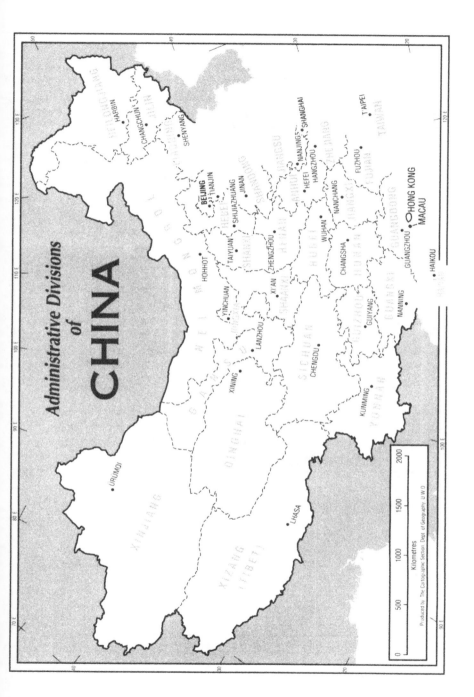

Map 1: The People's Republic of China

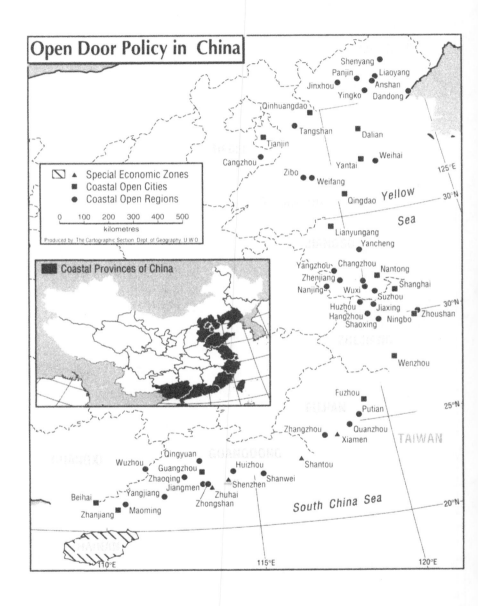

Map 2: China's Open Door Policy

1 Introduction

Introduction

This book is about the location of foreign direct investment (FDI) within a subnational context, with reference to the Chinese experience during 1979 to 1993. This chapter explains the subject, the nature, and the scope of this study.

China's 'open door' policy has caught enormous attention in the past ten years or so. It has been because China's opening has provided many opportunities and has had a noticeable impact on the world. The real implications of this new process in China's history will be in the years and decades to come. Indeed, China's opening to the West shows a dramatic change in the undercurrent running through China's thousands of years of history.

One aspect resulting from China's opening to the world is the inflow of foreign direct investment from developed countries, newly industrialized countries (NICs), and some developing countries. Out of a host of academically and practically challenging areas of studies related to foreign direct investment; this book sets out to deal with only one aspect: the spatial dimension of foreign direct investment.

This subject is easily justified within several contexts. As a destination for international direct capital flow, China's importance is second only to the United States, the world's largest economy. Also, China has been a planned economy. The presence of foreign direct investment that is mainly from the NICs and the West in China creates a unique area of study within the domain of international production. That is, international production within a major socialist economy. Most issues related to foreign direct investment in China would stand as separate fields of study on their own simply because of their uniqueness and practical importance. That, of course, includes the locational issue.

The research conducted by this study is also justified by its contribution to the theoretical understanding of the location of foreign direct investment within the subnational context. Such a comprehensive conceptual and theoretical framework has been lacking.

This research is also justified with the importance of foreign direct investment in China's economic development. Within the manufacturing industry, the gross output value of these enterprises invested in by foreigners accounted for close to 5 per cent of the national total in 1991. This was 8 per cent for the Coastal Open Cities, and 45 per cent for the four Special Economic Zones.

The definition of foreign direct investment and the scope of data coverage

Foreign direct investment and international portfolio investment are the dichotomous components in international capital flow. Portfolio investment is purely financial investment through the modality of the market. It does not entail control over the assets involved. Foreign direct investment, on the contrary, is international capital movement with the investing companies retaining the control over the use of the resources involved. It usually consists of a package of assets (Dunning, 1993, p. 5; Rugman, Lecraw, and Booth, 1985, p. 9).

The operational definition, though, varies from one country to another due to different assessments of effective control. The US Department of Commerce defines foreign direct investment as 'the movement of long term capital to finance business activity abroad, whereby investors control at least 10 per cent of the enterprise' (Ponioachek, 1986, p. 21). In Canada and other countries, this rate is usually higher than ten per cent (Rugman, Lecraw, and Booth, 1985, p. 9).

The operational definition of foreign direct investment used in this work, due to data constraints, covered a greater scope of enterprises. The Chinese government considers foreign investment in all the following four types of ventures as foreign direct investment:

1   wholly foreign owned ventures (WFVs),

2   equity joint ventures (EJVs),

3   cooperative joint ventures (CJVs), and

4   joint exploration ventures (JEVs).

In the earlier years of China's open door policy, this list also included processing and assembly arrangements plus compensation trade that now is included in the 'other FDI' category in government statistics.

JEVs are usually formed between the Chinese government and foreign oil companies to investigate offshore oil resources in China's sea territory. Both the total number and total amount of capital are negligible in the national total. As a result, foreign direct investment usually includes investment by the first three types of joint ventures that are collectively referred to as foreign invested ventures (FIVs) in this book.

While WFVs and EJVs are up to international standards in their definition, investments made by CJVs are a debatable category of foreign direct investment. In a CJV, a Chinese firm and a foreign firm, work together on a specific project usually with the Chinese side contributing mainly in kind, normally land or buildings, and the foreign investors contribute technology and capital. Profits are distributed according to a formula specified in their contracts. Because of the vague definition (in fact, the law governing CJVs was not published until early in 1988), in practice many such ventures have been treated as EJVs. This venture type was important in earlier years primarily for investors from Hong Kong. Its role as a dominant mode of entry in terms of contract numbers ceased after 1985. Nevertheless, it was an important vehicle for both local authorities and foreign investors to learn to cooperate and explore future opportunities.

Major objectives of this study

This work is about the location of foreign direct investment within a subnational context and the Chinese experience. As an objective and as a necessity to precede the empirical analysis of the spatial dimension of foreign direct investment in China, a comprehensive conceptual and theoretical framework for the location of foreign direct investment with a subnational context is built. Such a framework should be comprehensive and dynamic, within which various locational issues of foreign direct investment can be addressed.

The second objective is to uncover the locational determinants of foreign direct investment in China, not only as an empirical case study but also as a special area of study within the domain of foreign direct investment because of its importance and uniqueness. The general location patterns are not expected to be stationary, but will change through time. These changes represent nothing short of a dynamic process between foreign investors on one hand and host cities on the other. Within this dynamic context, the changes of the model, that are the changes of factors and variables about the location of foreign direct investment as whole, are discussed.

If the second objective is to answer the question of what makes one host city/region more attractive than another, the third objective of this book is to answer what causes foreign investors to prefer some cities to others as possible locations for their investment. It is really a question about the presence of foreign direct investment, rather than the spatial distribution of foreign direct investment (in actual amount or number of contracts). To answer this question, a distinction is made between cities that have foreign direct investment of varying amounts (FDI recipient city) and cities that have no foreign direct investment presence (FDI void city).

When compared with investments made by national firms, foreign direct investment represents a distinct category. However, this does not mean foreign direct investment is a homogeneous category. In fact, it can be further differentiated by its country of origin, size, and competitive strategy. It is out of the reach of this study to examine all the aspects of this diversity. Rather, this research aims to uncover only the country

3

of origin effect, i.e., the locational deviation of foreign direct investment because of its country of origin.

Structure of this book

This book proceeds in the following fashion. After the literature review on the main foreign direct investment theories, location theories and corporate geography, plus the empirical research on the location of foreign direct investment in Chapter Two, a conceptual and theoretical framework for the location of foreign direct investment at the subnational level is built in Chapter Three. This framework is a result of a process that involves critical selection of existing theories and studies and combining them into a hybrid framework. Chapter Four is a descriptive analysis of the overall process of foreign direct investment involvement in China since 1979 within the context of China's policy changes toward a more liberal investment environment. It provides not only some critical background information and an overview of the process, but also some inputs that are used later. Vigorous statistical modelling and analyzes mark Chapters Five, Six, and Seven. They are based on the comprehensive conceptual framework and achieve the stated objectives. While the presence of foreign direct investment is the focus of Chapter Five, Chapter Six aims at the general location pattern, the spatial distribution of foreign direct investment, and its change over time. Chapter Seven dissects one of the three dimensions of the conceptual framework, the effect of country of origin on location patterns of foreign direct investment. Chapter Eight concludes this work by summarizing the main results and proposing areas of further research.

2 The location of FDI: a literature review

Introduction

This chapter delves into a wealth of literature on foreign direct investment, both theories, empirical studies, and corporate geography, to uncover the locational mechanisms of foreign direct investment. A comprehensive locational framework for the location of foreign direct investment seems lacking. In the process of the unraveling of the key components of the major foreign direct investment theories, it is shown that corporate geography can contribute to the building of a conceptual and theoretical framework to accommodate the location of foreign direct investment. All the major strands of foreign direct investment theories, e.g., the market imperfection approach, the internationalization approach, the product cycle theory, the eclectic paradigm, and the macroeconomic approaches, are discussed.

The lack of a complete locational theory for foreign direct investment has not prevented empirical investigation on location related issues of foreign direct investment, e.g., the overall spatial patterns and locational determinants (factors). Two groups of studies of varying spatial units contribute to our understanding of the locational aspects of foreign direct investment:

1   survey studies and empirical analysis of determinants of foreign direct investment among countries, and

2   studies of the location of foreign direct investment within one country or geographical region.

The differences between these two groups are mainly in their foci, with the first group focusing on distribution of foreign direct investment within an international context and the latter on a subnational spatial context.

In this chapter, theories on foreign direct investment are discussed first, followed by a brief review of corporate geography's contributions. The empirical analysis on the location of foreign direct investment is reviewed at the end of this chapter.

Conventional theories of foreign direct investment and their locational implication

The market imperfections approach and industrial organization

The market imperfections approach (Hymer, 1976; Kindleberger, 1969; Caves, 1971, 1974b, 1974c; Calvet, 1981) starts with the basic assumption that without market imperfections foreign direct investment would never occur. Market imperfections can be caused by both goods and factor markets, scale economies, and government imposed regulations (especially tariff and trade barriers) that prevent the efficient allocation of resources and distribution of products. In a perfect market, the only vehicle needed to serve a foreign market is international trade.

It was also recognized that foreign direct investment is far different from portfolio investment. In the first place, foreign direct investment is more than just the transfer of capital, it is the transfer of a package of assets that includes technology, managerial skills, and access to international markets. Second, there is no change of ownership in the process. Multinational enterprises (MNEs) internalize the market by directly controlling the resources acquired with foreign direct investment. As such, portfolio capital theory that is based on the interest rate is insufficient to explain the movement of direct investment.

If an MNE intends to pursue foreign value-added activities, it is perceived to face some disadvantages in comparison with indigenous firms, e.g., the information cost concerning the operation of firms within a foreign social, institutional, and political system. To overcome the inherent disadvantages of owning international production, MNEs must possess some kind of ownership advantage. These perceived ownership advantages can be expressed as technology, cost effectiveness, established markets, and financial strength. Clearly, this assumption is along the line of reasoning in industrial organization theory where firm behavior is affected by market structure.

Many scholars have explored what kinds of firm characteristics and in what kinds of industries MNEs are prone to international production (Horst, 1972; Caves, 1974a; Hirsch, 1976; Lall, 1980). It was found that ownership specific advantages usually rest on intangible assets created by large firms with intensive research and development activity. This points to the high technology industries such as chemicals, pharmaceuticals, and instruments. Industries in mature oligopolies with higher seller concentration and higher barriers to entry also tend to play an important role in international production.

Although the market imperfections approach to foreign direct investment does not have a spatial dimension, it is important for our understanding of the characteristics of foreign direct investment. It aids us in understanding the locational mechanism of foreign direct investment, as any locational choice made by an MNE is one of the

6

responses that it makes within a dynamic environment concerning its own ownership specific advantages and competitive strategies.

Product cycle theory

Vernon's product cycle model is an integrated model for international trade and investment (1966, 1979). Three basic assumptions are made in Vernon's product cycle hypothesis. First, the monopolistic advantages enable MNEs to take on the special costs and uncertainties of direct production abroad. Second, there are marked differences between the markets and factor conditions of home and host countries. Third, a new product or innovation possessed by an MNE is stimulated by the promises of its home market.

Once a product is created through innovation, it is destined to go through a process of several stages from a new product to a mature product to a standardized product. Along this sequence, the specific aspects of monopolistic advantages that an MNE possesses change. So do the market demand, market structure, and the scale of production. Most important, in response to these changes and the differences in the factor conditions between host and home markets, the modes for the MNE to exploit its firm specific advantages change from export from the home market to direct production in host countries. Though there have been tremendous changes in the landscape of international production, the product cycle hypothesis remains relevant in explaining international trade and investment (Vernon, 1979), especially when it comes to the foreign direct investment from developed to developing countries.

Product cycle theory distinguishes itself from other theories in two aspects: its dynamic nature and its explicit locational dimension. The driving force in this dynamic process is innovation and technological progress. Yet, depending on their positions in the product cycle, MNEs adopt different strategies. Later, this was explicitly explored within a framework of three kinds of oligopolies: innovation-based, mature, and senescent oligopolies (Vernon, 1974). For the innovation-oriented industries, the oligopolistic strength of MNEs is through the development and introduction of new products and the differentiation of existing ones as results of high expenditure on research and development. The location of research and development facilities and production both would remain at a home market.

As for MNEs in mature oligopolies, the basis for oligopoly shifts to the barriers to entry generated by economies of scale in production or marketing. The major locational concern is just the location of production units, which can be affected by the pricing conventions among oligopolists, aggressive behavior of some competitors, or external factors. While the pricing conventions such as basing point systems strengthen the existing location patterns of MNEs' production, the aggressive behavior of some competitors is more likely to change them. In the case of a leading firm, the intruder moves into another one's (the rival) territory. The most likely response from the rival would be a countermove into the intruder's main market. When a leading firm moves into a new market for reasons like tariff and/or market potential, the 'following the leader' (Knickerbocker, 1973) practice would be employed by other firms in the industry. The spatial implication, in either case, would be the spread of production internationally.

Within senescent oligopolies, however, MNEs can no longer hold on to either innovation or scale economies advantages. They depend on competitive costs and prices to hold market share. MNEs tend to move their production to low-cost areas, such as developing countries. The locational behavior of MNEs within a given developing country, then, is more relevant to the classical locational model with the exception that the availabilities of some production factors such as capital are not restricted to local markets.

One aspect of the product cycle theory deserves special attention: that of the ownership advantages sourced from the home market. This assertion surfaces in Dunning's eclectic paradigm as the location-specific advantages of home countries. This relationship between MNEs and home countries is extensively discussed by Porter (1990) within the context of national competitiveness. In his view, each country's competitiveness that is usually represented by the successful expansion in foreign countries is derived from four types of home conditions:

1   factor conditions,

2   demand conditions,

3   related and supporting industries, and

4   firm strategy, structure, and rivalry.

Internalization approach

The internalization approach (Buckley and Casson, 1991; Buckley, 1988) represents a distinct shift from the market imperfection approach in that MNEs are approached within the context of the theory of the firm, the economics of internal organization. The focus then is not to explain why or how a firm pursues international production, but it is to build a theory of the MNE as an organization.

It is a fact that the modern business sector carries out a series of interrelated economic activities that form a value added chain. Between the two modes of transaction - market and hierarchy - it is often found that the latter is superior to the former in organizing the intermediate products due to market imperfections. The cost efficiency of exchange and transaction through a hierarchy urges firms to bypass the market and create an internal market that brings the related intermediate product markets and production under common ownership and control. Such MNEs are the result of the process of internationalization of markets across national boundaries.

Clearly, the internalization theory of MNEs explains why MNEs chose to take joint ownership of both domestic and foreign value-added activities. But it does not explain clearly why MNEs participate in international production in the first place. In this respect, the explanation has to rely on the assumptions espoused by the market imperfection approach. As it will be clear later in the discussion of the eclectic paradigm, this still is not sufficient. The locational advantages of both home and host nation also must be present to allow international production to occur.

The eclectic paradigm

Dunning's eclectic approach (Dunning, 1979; 1980; 1988a; 1993) represents the state of the art in explaining international production. Alternative theories of foreign direct investment look into foreign direct investment from different specific perspectives. For example, the market imperfections approach explains why international production happens and what ownership specific advantages MNEs possess. The internalization approach, based on the theory of the firm, explains the ownership characteristics of international production. The eclectic approach, however, represents the most recent theoretical endeavor to bring these alternative perspectives together within one framework. Yet, the eclectic paradigm is not just a simple compiling of different strands of theories. Each alternative theory is brought in to explain both the location and ownership characteristics of international production. As Dunning puts it, 'The theory of the determinants of MNE activity must then seek to explain both the location of value-adding activities, and the ownership and organization of these activities' (Dunning, 1993, p. 66).

The basic hypothesis of the eclectic paradigm is that international production only occurs when there is a juxtaposition of three types of advantages related to a specific firm: ownership-specific advantages (O), location-specific advantages (L), and market internalization advantages (I). This produces 'OLI' as an abbreviation for the eclectic paradigm.

The first condition for international production obviously is adopted from the market imperfection approach that asserts an MNE must possess some ownership advantage. These advantages largely take the form of intangible assets that can be manifested in technology, product differentiation, or managerial skills. As for the source of these advantages, Dunning borrows the idea first espoused by Vernon (1966), that is, firm specific advantages originate from the process of serving home country markets. In other words, it is the home country's endowments and market characteristics that cause firm specific advantages. Although these firm specific advantages were linked to location-specific endowments during the process of their creation, they are not confined to a specific location or to a specific user once they are created. However, they may still be exclusive and specific to the firm that creates them. With this kind of impact that country-specific characteristics can exert on MNEs in mind, Dunning cautions the generalization of international production from one country to another.

A second necessary condition for international production is the presence of location-specific advantages in host countries. International production will not occur if it is unprofitable to use at least one factor input with a firm's ownership advantages. Here the relevance of location theory in international production is acknowledged, as is the pervasiveness of uneven distribution of both resources and markets.

Even with O and L advantages, international production still will not occur if it were not for the advantages of internalizing the use of O advantages. It is here that

9

the theory of firm and the internalization approach to international production come into play in Dunning's OLI paradigm. MNEs enter foreign production only when it is beneficial to exploit the O advantages themselves rather than relinquish them to the markets.

Dunning's OLI paradigm is especially relevant to this book on two accounts. First, it has an explicit spatial and locational dimension in explaining international production. Location is an integral part of inducing foreign direct investment, not just relevant to the locational choices for the production sites. Second, this framework is by far the most comprehensive and robust.

Macroeconomic approach

This line of approach is usually identified with Kojima (1982). It is stated that the flow of foreign direct investment originates from the comparative disadvantages of home countries and the potential comparative advantages of host countries regarding certain industries. Kojima calls it 'the principle of DFI (direct foreign investment) originating in the marginal (including submarginal) industry' (p. 2, 1982).

Kojima's macroeconomic approach can be distinguished from other approaches in several aspects. First, it intends to integrate international trade and foreign direct investment. Second, due to its foundation from comparative advantage, it is more flexible and all-embracing. While other approaches discuss most issues in absolute terms, the macroeconomic theory of foreign direct investment approaches relevant issues in a comparative fashion between one country and another. Also, while there is usually only one industry within the framework of other theories, the macroeconomic approach embraces at least two commodities or industries, which is typically shown by the international trade model.

Third, the industries of foreign direct investment identified by macroeconomic approach are trade-oriented and complement rather than hinder international trade, at least theoretically. As these industries are usually marginal industries in home countries, the production of these industries in host countries will lead to the import of new products from host countries. This is directly contrary to other approaches that identify foreign direct investment originating from industries with oligopolistic advantages that essentially are anti-trade-oriented. Fourth, the notion of marginal industry can be readily substituted with marginal production without any necessary modification and losing its explanatory power. In this sense, it is more flexible.

The macroeconomic approach to foreign direct investment tends to explain foreign direct investments as what they might be, not as what they are. This theory also tends to perpetuate the dependent relationships that developing countries have on developed countries. However, this theory is not without merit. When it comes to the foreign direct investment from home countries that are experiencing structural transformation, the macroeconomic approach may be more appropriate than others in explaining the characteristics of the outflow of foreign direct investment (Buckley, 1983).

10

Geography of large enterprises

Corporate spatial system: spatial organization of corporate production

This strand of research has been based on the spatial separation of functional units of large corporations (Walker, 1988). Large corporations consist of certain interconnected activities within the complex chain of production and distribution of one or more commodities. All the activities in a large corporation that straddle local, regional, and national boundaries make up the 'company region' McNee (1974). A company region is obviously a planning region within which coordination and direction supersede market interaction. Corporate geographers have paid attention to the multiplicity of ways in which the elements in the value-added chain may be organized in space, plus the chain's implications.

The hierarchical organizational structure of large organizations is obviously a starting point for the general pattern of a corporate spatial system. It has been found that the control (Bochert, 1978; Burns, 1977; Goddard, 1975; Rees, 1978a)and research and development (Malecki, 1978, 1979) functions have been predominantly located in larger metropolitan areas and the most prosperous regions. Branch plants with standardized technology and equipment tend to be in low labor cost regions. This hierarchical corporate spatial system is strongly implied by the product cycle applied at a regional scale. This spatial relationship is not that different from general patterns observed between regions, between cities of different sizes, and between an urban area and its hinterland in urban geography and the regional economic development literature.

While most researchers adopted conventional economic and organizational views on corporate behavior, others took a radical Marxist perspective (Massey, 1978, 1979; Massey and Meegan, 1979; Storper and Walker, 1983; Walker and Storper, 1981). The corporate enterprise is considered an inappropriate unit of analysis, as its behavior can only be understood within the context of the whole capitalist economic system, especially within the context of the conflict between capital and labor. From this perspective, the spatial form of the hierarchical structure of large corporations is seen as a locational hierarchy where there is 'a spatial division of labor between, for instance, research, development and initial production on the one hand and fully finalized mass production on the other' (Massey and Meegan, 1979, p. 107). The central issue of the idea of locational hierarchy is about the spatial distribution of control on production.

By examining the spatial form of an MNE's resources and the flow of information and materials, a core-periphery structure can usually be discerned in a corporate spatial system (McNee, 1974; Rees, 1974; Blackbourn, 1974). Within the 'core', which is usually in a large metropolitan area, functional units such as production plants, offices, and other facilities are closely interrelated by the flows of information, technology, materials, and services. Operations outside the core form the periphery of large corporations. For MNEs, their peripheries are usually foreign operations in other markets. Between the core and the periphery, however, the most frequent linkages are informational and personnel. It is also noted that because of the

11

friction caused by either distance or social and cultural distance, the periphery of a large corporation, especially that of an MNE, is usually a subsystem which not only enjoys a high level of autonomy, but also provides feedbacks to the core.

Locational decision making

Definition and frequency of locational decision making

Although conscious and explicit locational policies are usually found only in large and market oriented corporations, it has been established that all business decisions have locational components and implications (McNee, 1974; North, 1974; Rees, 1974; Stafford, 1974). As Hamilton puts it, 'for many firms and many types of business decisions, the locational aspect is likely to a byproduct of a particular policy to achieve some nonspatial goal' (1974, p. 14). It appears that the frequency of the locational decision varies with firm size, growth rate, and complexity.

A general stimulus-response model of corporate decision making has been adopted by most corporate geographers for the initiation of locational decision making. The stress conditions may stem from both internal and external sources such as intra-firm maladjustment, firm performance, and maladjustment between the firm and its external environment. There is a range of options that firms can employ to deal with these stresses: branch plants (subsidiary), closure, in situ adjustment, merger and acquisition, and collaboration (joint venture) with other firms (Dicken and Lloyd, 1990; North, 1974). North (1974) further identifies the relationships between corporate stress conditions and the most likely avenues that firms are likely to take. For example, a branch plant is most likely to be identified with tapping into new regional markets. Obviously, each option that a firm takes is to achieve a multiple of goals such as growth, market expansion, or diversification of interests in pursuit of a reasonable level of profitability.

The organizational structure is also likely affect corporate strategy and actions (Chandler, 1962; Hamilton, 1974; Bower and Doz, 1979). Various organizational characteristics have a bearing on the power structure in an organization and thus conflict resolution.

The locational components in different business decisions are different in more than one way: the importance of locational factors and the spatial extent of a locational search (North, 1974). For in situ adjustment, there is no new locational search and the locational component in that decision is to compare the existing functional units. Branch plants are likely to incur the most extensive locational search within which locational factors may exert the most influence. There may be a limited locational search if a firm undertakes a merger or acquisition. More important, like the case of in situ adjustment, existing units or firms' performances may be a more important criterion than any other factors.

12

Locational decision making: a limited search process

Locational decision making has two interesting attributes. First, it is a non-operational decision (Pred, 1974). Second, because of the uncertainty in the environment, and limited and biased information available to corporate decision makers coupled with cost constraints (in both monetary and temporal terms) there is often only a limited search for locational alternatives (North, 1974; Rees, 1974; Stafford, 1974).

This limited search process involves two basic steps. At the macro level, i.e., choosing a region for plant location, the decision is usually made on judgmental factors without detailed study on the merits of all possible alternatives. In other words, this process is an impressionistic delimitation of the specific area for a more detailed locational evaluation. At the micro level, the locational decision is more in line with a cost minimization normative approach.

Spatial evolution of corporate spatial system

Paralleled with theories in industrial economics, corporate geographers also try to depict the relatively unimpeded trajectory of corporate growth in a spatial context (Taylor, 1975; Hakanson, 1977; McNee, 1974; Watts, 1980a). While corporate growth models in industrial economics focus on the constraints of corporate growth (Penrose, 1959), models in geography emphasize the internal structural metamorphosis associated with growth and its spatial manifestation.

The grounding of corporate spatial process lies in the basic corporate development sequence proposed by Chandler (1962) and Ansoff (1965). This sequence postulates that an enterprise goes through four distinct stages: market penetration, product development, market development, and diversification. As any production is not conducted on a pin head, the availability of various means of growth (internal versus external, vertical, horizontal), becomes an integral matter of corporate growth and organization.

The spatial outcome of the process is the creation of a core region around the corporation, followed by the interregional expansion of sale offices and production, and then international expansion by following the sequence of sale-assembly-production. In other words, the task environment of an enterprise is progressively extended from regional to national to international (Hamilton, 1974, p. 17).

The essence of corporate spatial evolution is a spatial learning process involving nested action spaces, information spaces, and decision spaces (Taylor and Thrift, 1982, p. 28). Thus, one may not ignore the direction of spatial expansion with reference to urban hierarchy. Both interregional and international expansions incline toward major market nodes, usually the first and second order cities in a country (Rees, 1974; Blackbourn, 1974). The explanation in part lies in the perceived zone of opportunity (McNee, 1974) which is heavily influenced by the circulation of information and diffusion of growth-inducing innovations (Pred, 1974).

However, this isolated view of individual corporate growth should be qualified considering the imperfect competition present in industries populated by large corporations. Case studies (Rees, 1978b; Watts, 1980a, 1980b) show that undisturbed spatial expansion paths of firms should be corrected by the oligopolistic reaction among competitors.

Firms and the environment

It has been realized that the behavior of large corporations can only be understood within the environment within which firms operate and survive. As complex and elusive as a firm's environment is, Hayter and Watts (1983) were correct in that three critical aspects should be dealt with regarding the firm's environment. These are:

1   the demarcation of firm and its environment,

2   relevant components in the environment, and

3   the firm-environment relationships.

By comparison, corporate geographers paid more attention to the relevancy of the components in its environment and the firm-environment relationships than to the definition of firm. Control of assets is usually implicitly the criteria for the definition of a firm, although suggestions have been made to extend the concept to that of a managed economic system (MacMillan and Farmer, 1978, p. 284).

Within the complexity of the environment that comprises 'many strata of different phenomena, of varying importance, (and) of varying temporal or spatial incidence' (Hamilton, 1974, p. 26), corporate geographers have been pragmatic in selecting relevant components from the total objective environment. In fact, this has been a tradition since classical locational theories (Weber, 1929) when a firm's location problem is solved within the context of spatial variation of factors of production and markets. Other than these direct material linkages, government and social factors are also noted as relevant to locational decision making (Steed, 1971). In truth, this definition of locational environment is not fundamentally different from the task environment conceptualized in organization theory (Dill, 1958; Thompson, 1967). Task environment includes those organizations with which the focal organization (firm) establishes exchange relationships. These exchanges can assume the forms of materials, goods or information. Together, the organization forms an environment that is critical to the survival of the organization and its decision making.

With the issues such as the quality of information and the ability to use information outstanding, distinctions are also made between the perceived and objective environment (Pred, 1967; 1969). The perceived environment is determined by the coding mechanism (Dicken, 1971) and a function of managerial expectations, internal organizational structure and resources of the firm (Steed, 1971; Dicken, 1971; North; 1974, Rees; 1974).

The influence of competitors in the firm environment did not escape the attention of geographers (Steed, 1971). Following the principles established by Knickerbocker (1973), some studies explicitly take into account the impact of the oligopolistic behavior of firms (Watts, 1980a, 1980b; Rees, 1978c; McConnell, 1980). The explicit conceptualization of competitors as a component in a firm's environment by Emery and Trist (1965) was also adopted by geographers (McDermott and Taylor, 1982; Steed, 1971). In addition to placid and randomized, placid and clustered, and disturbed-reactive types of environment, which correspond respectively to perfect competition, imperfect competition, and oligopoly in economics, Emery and Trist also identified a fourth type, that is the turbulent environment. Clearly, within different types of environments, firms' tactics and strategies differ, so do their locational behavior and their relationships with the environment in terms of their impact on the environment.

As to the interdependencies between the firm and the environment, environment has been seen as a deterministic force in explaining firm behavior, from both the behavioral and structural approaches. Within corporate geography, a firm's behavior is largely explained as a purposive response to the stresses from its environment. This includes not only the initial locational decision, but also the process of adoption to its environment afterwards (Townroe, 1974; Lever, 1974; Gilmour, 1974; Britton, 1974). This process of adoption is possible due to internal changes, such as innovation. However, the most important causes are the dynamic changes in the environment and the imperfection in the firm's perception of its environment before the location choice.

The structural approach in corporate geography addresses the firm-environment relationship from a much different perspective (Massey, 1978, 1979; Massey and Meegan, 1979; Storper, 1981). By this approach, firms, representing the interests of capital, are considered parts of an overall system dominated by the capitalist mode of production. As such, a firm's behavior is a product of the overall structure of the system, and can only be explained by the long term shifts in the whole environment.

A critique of corporate geography

First, the dynamics between the firm and the environment have not been fully explored. Specifically, corporations' active role in changing their environment to their advantage is not acknowledged. Simply by realizing the adaptive nature of large firms (adopter) to their environment is not enough. One must also realize the role of technology overall and research and development in particular, in shaping the relationship between the firm and its environment. Demand is no longer simply an external factor, but also an internal factor in that corporate research and development and marketing to a certain extent create demand. Most important, is the ability of firms to internalize segments of the environment during their growth (Coase, 1937).

Second, corporate geography has been concentrating on a specific species in modern economy, that is the very large corporate enterprise, especially large MNEs. The development process and behavior of these enterprises may not be applicable to most present day firms such as small firms, larger national firms, and even small multinationals due to banking, finance, and other gaps (Taylor and Thrift, 1982, p.32).

Locational determinants of foreign direct investment inflow among countries[1]

Country-related factors influencing CEOs' locational decisions: results of survey studies

Dunning (1973) summarized the survey studies conducted before the 1970s which set out to identify the main country-related factors marked by business executives as important in their locational decision making. These decisions concern their strategic planning to invest abroad.

It was found that the goals of MNEs embarking on international production and the determinants that MNEs' executives take into account are mixed. Dunning distinguishes four major categories of factors influencing this business decision:

1   market factors which include not only market size and growth rate, but also the motives of MNEs such as maintaining market share and promoting the exports of parent companies;

2   trade barriers;

3   factors which influence the cost of production; and

4   the investment climate that consists of mainly such aspects as political stability, the general attitude toward foreign direct investment, and the incentives and disincentives in host countries.

As Dunning reports, the conclusions derived from these surveys seem clear. The most important factors in MNEs' executives perceptions are host governments' attitude toward inward foreign direct investment, political stability, and market sizes and their potential. Cost factors are least important in enticing MNEs to establish production abroad. Another characteristic about these studies besides their seemingly clear conclusions is their focus on economic factors that influence the investment decisions of MNEs. Political stability included in the investment climate represents the only one exception.

The limitation of these survey studies is also identified by Dunning (1973). First, these studies failed to distinguish between the motives and determinants of international production. Second, the same answer given by different firms may be interpreted differently and no attempt is made in these studies to analyze the assumptions underlying the answers given by firms. Third, they fail to normalize the differences between different firms or countries.

Determinants of the distribution of foreign direct investment among countries: results of empirical studies

This group of studies, although they also attack the question of why international production tends to be strong in some countries rather than others, stands out in stark contrast to the survey studies in several aspects. First, these studies are based on observations of realized foreign direct investment inflow rather than MNE's executives' perceptions. Second, the factors included in these studies encompass a broader range by including socio-economic factors in addition to political and economic factors. Furthermore, the conclusions derived from these studies are more convincing in a sense that they are established on cross-national statistical analysis. Studies in this group can be further grouped into three different categories:

1   those that focus on the environmental determinants of foreign direct investment from one country (Scaperlanda and Mauer, 1969; Korbin, 1976; Koechlin, 1992; Chen, 1992; Yeon, 1992),

2   studies on the factors that influence the total inflow of foreign direct investment in developing countries (Reuber, 1973; Root and Ahmed, 1979; Schneider and Frey, 1985), and

3   studies on one or several major environmental factors (Lim, 1983).

Scaperlanda and Mauer's study (1969) was among the first to divert attention from descriptive analysis to statistically testing the importance of determinants of foreign direct investment inflow. Three principal hypotheses were postulated regarding determinants of foreign direct investment inflow: market size, economic growth, and tariff discrimination. By testing US foreign direct investment in the EEC from 1952 to 1966 against these three variables, only market size was statistically significant.

Korbin's study (1976) was more comprehensive in factors considered, although tariff factors were not included. Major groups of factors were identified by using factor analysis. They consist of: social and economic variables, market size and market growth; and political factors such as rebellion, instability, and subversion. By regressing US manufacturing investment as of year-end 1967 on the six factor groups, market size was the overriding determinant with social economic development and market growth as the second and third statistically significant factors. All three political factor groups failed the test, and some even had negative coefficients.

A recent study by Koechlin (1992) confirms the relevancy of both social, political and economic variables in the determining the location of US outward foreign direct investment. The real inflow of US foreign direct investment in manufacturing to host countries between 1966 and 1985 was regressed against a host of country-related variables. Three economic models (the cost model, the demand model, and a hybrid economic model) were tested first. Koechlin further constructed a political-economic model by adding three political variables into the hybrid economic model. One is Business Environment Risk index that captures the political stability of host countries and attitudes toward foreign investment. The other two represent the dependence of host countries on the US and the language of host countries. The comparison between the economic models and the political-economic model shows that the latter was the best in explaining the distribution of US foreign direct investment among countries.

While the above three studies shed light on the determinants of foreign direct investment from developed countries, Yeon's study (1992) reveals distinct features of the determinants of foreign direct investment from newly industrializing countries such as South Korea. Foreign direct investment from South Korea to developed countries may be motivated by a desire to evade nontariff trade barriers. Direct investment that went to lesser developed countries, on the other hand, may be driven mainly by the comparative cost advantages in developing countries, especially the cheap labor.

Instead of using regression analysis like most of the studies mentioned above, Root and Ahmed's study (1979) employed discriminant analysis to identify major factors influencing foreign direct investment inflow among three major country groups classified as unattractive, attractive, and highly attractive for annual per capita inflow of foreign direct investment during 1966 to 1970 in 70 countries. Among 37 different economic, social, and political factors, each appeared at least once in previous empirical studies, only six emerge as essential discriminators. They include per capita gross domestic product (GDP); GDP growth rate; economic integration; extent of urbanization; commerce, transport and communication; and regular executive transfers calculated for 1956 to 1967. Although the only political factor (regular executive transfer), failed to distinguish among the three country groups during 1960 to 1970, it is argued that foreign investors view political stability from a long-term perspective.

Schneider and Frey (1985) employed a similar approach to Koechlin's (1992) to study the locational determinants of total foreign direct investment among countries. The conclusions of both studies are also similar in that a political-economic model is found performing best in explaining the international distribution of foreign direct investment. The difference between these two studies, though, is reflected in the differences between their economic models and political factors included in their political-economic models. Among the political determinants, the amount of bilateral aid from Western countries was found to have the strongest stimulating effect by Schneider and Frey, while aid from communist countries was found to have significant negative effects.

Unlike most others, Lim's (1983) study paid more attention to the impact of the fiscal incentives on the distribution of foreign direct investment in less developed countries. The hypothesis that greater generosity of fiscal incentives attracts more foreign direct investment is clearly rejected by statistical tests. This finding confirms Reuber's (1973) discussion on the impact of incentives on the inflow of foreign direct investment. While the incentives in developing countries clearly tend to be ever more generous resulting from the competition among them, their overall impact on foreign direct investment is marginal. However, fiscal incentives may be important to small firms whose market behavior is short-sighted compared with large firms (Reuber, 1973; Lim, 1983).

The fact that developing countries still use incentives extensively though there is proof of their ineffectiveness to attract foreign direct investment presents an 'apparent paradox' (Lim, 1983, p. 210). One possible explanation for this is that it is the intention of developing countries to compete with each other and/or to compensate for their lack of resources and other factors that determine the inflow of foreign direct investment. Another explanation is offered by Agarwal (1980) who argues that the effect of incentives may be well canceled by the regulatory disincentives such as restrictions on ownership or export performance.

While most studies mentioned above discuss the spatial distribution of accumulated foreign direct investment over time, Edgington's (1995) recent study focuses on the impact of a regional trade block (NAFTA) on the allocation of foreign direct investment in Canada. Trade liberalization indeed can provide greater locational flexibility for MNEs, yet whether to take advantage of the opportunity provided by regional integration to move their production abroad depends on several factors. First, it depends on firm specific advantages and product characteristics. Price sensitive products and labor intensive industries may be geared to less developed areas such as Mexico to take advantage of cheap labor costs. High technology production may just stay where it is. Second, the level of integration between an MNE's production and host economy also plays an important role. A well integrated MNE production facility is unlikely to be moved.

Evaluation of studies on locational determinants of foreign direct investment within the national context

Compared with the survey studies, the conclusions drawn from empirical analyzes have several distinct features. First, market factors especially market size, rather than political factors such as political stability, are unequivocally recognized as the overriding determinants of the distribution of foreign direct investment among countries. Factors representing levels of social and economic development are second in their importance in inducing foreign direct investment. It appears there is a contradiction between executives' perception of factors influencing foreign direct investment decisions and the variables that condition the distribution of foreign direct investment. Second, an incoherent picture is presented concerning the importance of other factors, e.g., political stability, cost factors and other economic indicators such as economic growth.

The seeming conflicts between the results of these studies should be viewed within the following context. Obviously, different data sets, methodologies and operational definitions were employed in different studies, which had important impacts on their findings. For political factors, there is an inherent bias in these studies (Korbin, 1976) in that only countries that received substantial foreign direct investment inflow were included in these studies, which means only positive investment decisions were studied. Political factors may play an important role in MNEs' initial screening process among countries (Stobaugh, 1969) and the production decision was made only among politically acceptable countries. The definitional differences about political factors are evident from the above review.

The conclusions from most of these studies should be taken with caution for two other reasons. Most of these studies were conducted in the 1970s and early 1980s, a period during which foreign direct investment was predominately conducted by western developed countries, especially the United States. As Yeon's (1992) study suggests, foreign direct investment from other countries especially NICs that are an increasingly important source of foreign direct investment outflow, may have distinct characteristics for the determinants of its distribution. Incentives and cost factors may play an important role in its location. Another reason is that all these studies were aimed at exposing the determinants of foreign direct investment as a totality, but they failed to capture the diversity of foreign direct investment for different types of investment. While cost factors were considered less important in both survey studies and empirical analysis, Riedel (1976) found that low wage costs have been a major determinant of export-oriented foreign direct investment in Taiwan.

The survey and empirical studies reviewed above have been on the locational aspects of foreign direct investment. The focus is obviously placed within an international context. Geographical locational factors are absent from these studies due to their nature. Nevertheless, the implications of the findings from these works on studying the spatial distribution of foreign direct investment within a subnational context should not be ignored. The influence of market factors and social economic factors within an international context may be carried over to the location of foreign direct investment within a country. While some factors such as political factors may be safely assumed away, other factors such as incentives and cost may assume more important roles. Of course, locational factors such as distance may emerge as additional important determinants of the spatial distribution of foreign direct investment within a specific country.

Spatial distribution of foreign direct investment within a subnational context

While a substantial body of research has been devoted to the identification and explanation of international flow of capital investment, only recently has attention been explicitly extended to the locational aspects of foreign direct investment on the subnational level. The body of literature generated from this undertaking is less sizable, yet not lacking important findings. This small body of literature mainly involves empirical analysis of regional distribution of foreign direct investment in the United States and the United Kingdom based on aggregate data from government sources. Regional variables being tested vary from one study to another.

Spatial distribution of foreign direct investment in the United States

McConnell (1980; 1983) was among the first to deal with the spatial distribution of foreign direct investment on a subnational level. The oligopolistic-reaction model of foreign investment stipulates that firms follow the leaders in their respective industries to reduce the risks and maintain the momentum established by the leaders. The hypothesis put forth by McConnell (1980) based on this model is that the location behavior of foreign affiliates should 'be strongly influenced by the locational force and industrial patterns that are already prevailing in the country' (p. 263). However, this hypothesis does not live up to empirical testing using 1974 to 1978 data. There was a dissimilarity between the foreign firms and domestic firms in 1976. The spatial pattern of foreign direct investment may be well explained by a host of traditional predictors of industrial location such as agglomeration economies, urban density, and economic-shadow effect. The presumed adverse effects of high union membership, high wages, population decline, and the absence of local incentives are not evident in the model. The locational pattern of foreign direct investment did not appear to reflect the mechanism of the regional shift of American manufacturing industry, in which factors such as personal and corporate taxes, climate, labor cost and unionization played important roles. McConnell concludes that foreign direct investment in the US, although it started to disperse from the industrial heartland, still lagged behind the regional shift of American industry overall. McConnell (1983) further examined the geographical dispersion of foreign direct investment at the sub-state level. He found that it is closely correlated with the population size and the number of research and development facilities of US private corporations.

Lauger and Shetty's (1985) conditional logit analysis of 76 new plant start-ups in three industries among states reveals the positive effects of agglomeration economies and state policies. It is not surprising that labor cost as reflected in wages deter the inflow of foreign direct investment.

Moore, Steece, and Swenson's (1987) study concerns net foreign direct investment in manufacturing assets among states. Regression analyzes reveal that favorable business climate, population, and labor supply have encouraged MNE investment. Taxation, on the other hand, exerts a negative impact on MNEs' investment commitments.

Bagchi-Sen and Wheeler (1989) developed a spatial and temporal model of foreign direct investment in the United States. Based on the hypothesis that the locational advantages of the US for foreign firms are the size of local and regional markets and proximity to skilled labor and technology, the population size, population growth rate, and per capita sales are selected as major independent variables to test against the inflow of foreign direct investment in metropolitan areas within the United States. Besides finding that all these parameters are positively related to the accumulation of foreign direct investment in a metropolitan region, Bagchi-Sen and Wheeler also showed the variations of the model over space and time.

Glickman and Woodward's (1988) study concluded that the agglomeration effect, labor climate, and transportation and urbanization are the most important variables in explaining the spatial distribution of foreign direct investment. However, the change of energy cost that is 'a central factor in recent shifts of manufacturing capital to the South and West' (p. 149) should also be included in the explanation of the change of foreign direct investment over space. They also dispute the argument that domestic investment follows foreign investment or vice versa (McConnell, 1980 and 1983; Ó hUallacháin, 1985a) and conclude that foreign and domestic investment locational determinants are just becoming similar.

A recent study by Coughlin, Terza and Arromdee (1991) updates our knowledge concerning the spatial pattern of foreign direct investment in the US. First, this study confirms the strong association of existing manufacturing activity density, population, and extensive infrastructures and promotional expenditure with inflow of foreign direct investment. Second, this study detects other factors such as taxes and labor cost

21

that have bearings on the location of foreign direct investment within the United States. These factors either were not included in some studies mentioned above or found statistically insignificant. One should note that the statistical insignificance of these factors in McConnell's test was the main reason for his conclusion that there was evident dissimilarity between the locational behavior of foreign affiliates and domestic firms in the US. Finally, it provides some evidence to support Glickman and Woodward's (1988) assertion that the location behaviors of foreign firms and domestic firms converge over time.

Woodward's (1992) empirical analysis on Japanese affiliated manufacturing investment, unlike other empirical studies, simulates the location choice of MNE investment at two spatial scales: state and county. At the state level, per capita income, the unionization rate, taxes, and macro-geographic location are important location factors. At the county level, manufacturing agglomeration, population density, infrastructure, and labor supply were found relevant. It is noteworthy that the factors at these two spatial levels are different, which may prove the hypothesis that location decision in general is a search process involving distinct stages (Haigh, 1989).

One more recent study by Ondrich and Wasylenko (1993) further confirms the results of previous studies. MNE investment was driven by the market size, agglomeration economies, and, to a lesser extent, cost and fiscal factors.

Spatial distribution of foreign direct investment in the UK

Unlike their US counterparts, studies in the UK put more emphasis on the overall spatial patterns of foreign direct investment without revealing the major underlying locational factors (Dicken and Lloyd, 1976; McDermott, 1977; Watts, 1979, 1980b; Law, 1980). Nevertheless, the conclusions from these studies are more coherent than the studies in the United States. Before the 1950s, foreign direct investment was heavily concentrated in the South East, the industrial core of the British economy. However, a continuing shift away from the core was discerned in the 1960s and early 1970s. Because of this process, foreign direct investment in the UK was over represented in both the South East and the assisted regions, leaving intermediate regions under represented.

This pattern of spatial distribution of foreign direct investment seems to show that the location behavior of British firms differs from foreign firms as a whole with foreign firms showing a distinct bias in favor of less developed regions. One reason for the different location behavior, as Law (1980) suggested, may be that foreign firms are generally more sensitive to the incentives available in the peripheral areas.

The aggregate behavior of foreign firms does not suggest that the locational behavior of foreign direct investment of different source countries is identical. As Watts (1979, 1980a, 1980b) proved, there are distinct differences between foreign direct investment from the US and from the EEC. While foreign direct investment from the US basically represents the overall pattern of foreign direct investment in the UK, foreign direct investment from the EEC is more localized than both British firms and foreign direct investment from the US and concentrated in nonassisted regions with significant concentration in the South East. Regional policies in assisted regions did not seem to have an impact on the locational behavior of the EEC firms. Blackbourn's study (1972) on the location of foreign-owned manufacturing plants in Ireland also found significant differences of locational preferences among different national groups.

Rather than identifying the spatial pattern of foreign direct investment in the UK, Hill and Munday (1992) tried to uncover the factors underlying the spatial distribution of foreign direct investment in the UK. The effectiveness of a regional infrastructure (which is treated as a surrogate of access to market) and financial incentives are important to the regional distribution of new foreign direct investment projects and jobs. Considering the recent nature of the data set (1980s) used in this study, it may be concluded that the general shift identified by the studies above is a continuing phenomenon. The agent for this continuing shift is new foreign direct investment directed toward peripheral regions.

Evaluation of studies on spatial distribution of foreign direct investment within a subnational context

First, most studies are done based on conventional locational theories aimed at identification of the relationship between locational attributes and foreign direct investment. Although these empirical studies may have different results, they do not invalidate one another. The different results of these studies show that the conclusions drawn about the spatial dimension of foreign direct investment may mirror the differences of their methodology, data type (employment, number of plants, value-invested), and time period used in their studies. Combined, all these studies may provide a useful picture of the spatial distribution pattern of foreign direct investment within one country over time and at different spatial scales.

Second, as the results from these studies are different to a certain extent, one is left without a concrete model to tackle the spatial dimension of foreign direct investment. However, given a myriad of factors lying behind the regional dimension of inward foreign direct investment, several factors (e.g., existing manufacturing establishment, market potential, infrastructure, labor) consistently show up as important influences in shaping the landscape of regional distribution of inward foreign direct investment.

Third, foreign direct investment concentrates in major metropolitan regions as evidenced from the US studies. The United Kingdom is an exception with foreign direct investment over represented in both core and periphery regions and under represented in the intermediate regions. This may suggest that there are differences of spatial distribution patterns of foreign direct investment within different spatial scales. The UK may represent the distribution of foreign direct investment on a sub-state spatial level as compared with the United States.

A fourth conclusion that can be drawn from these studies is that foreign firms of different country origins may respond differently to the national space in a particular economy. McConnell (1983) ascribes the geographic proximity, long history of presence, and inertia to spatial spread as the reasons for the location preferences of

Canadian, British, and Japanese foreign direct investment, respectively. Within the context of Britain and Ireland, where spatial scales constrain the richness of location behavior of MNEs, distinctions between different locational preferences of different source countries are made between the preference for less developed regions or central developed regions. Unfortunately, these studies did not provide a concrete explanation to this interesting phenomenon. Apart from behavior associated with different cultures, the difference in industry types, firm size, and entry methods may also contribute to explanation of this observation.

Finally, regarding this research, conclusions drawn from these studies should be viewed with caution. Some studies clearly show that the motives of inward foreign direct investment in the US are different from those in developing countries (Vernon, 1971; Arpan and Ricks, 1974; Ajami and Ricks, 1981). The striking difference is that foreign direct investment in the US is strongly motivated to gain access to US technology that is not a motive for foreign direct investment in developing countries. The spatial implication of these different motives is yet to be discovered.

Empirical studies on the location of foreign direct investment in China

Because the literature on foreign direct investment in China is scarce, in-depth studies are few. Most of the literature focuses on trying to introduce to the West the basics about China such as the policy, the systems, the economic reality, and how to do business in China. Several studies among this body of literature to be recommended are those on joint ventures (Shan, 1991; Beamish and Wang, 1989; Conley and Beamish, 1986; Tao, 1988), those on China's trade system (Shan, 1989), those on SEZs (Chu and Wong, 1986), those on China's investment environment (Ruggles, 1983), and those on the spatial aspect of the impact of China's economic reform (Xie and Costa, 1991).

Scholarly effort on the locational characteristics and the locational mechanism is lacking. This is not only because of the newness of the issue, but also because of data constraints. Most, if not all, of the handful of studies rely on a small database that includes 1676 joint ventures signed during 1979 to 1985. Three descriptive studies (Xie and Dutt, 1993; Leung, 1990; and Schroath, Yu, and Chen, 1993) based on this joint venture list provide the most useful information on general location patterns of foreign direct investment in China before 1986. It was found that:

1   foreign direct investment was disproportionally distributed in east coastal regions and larger urban centers,

2   the location of foreign direct investment was also affected by the social and kinship relationships between investors and host regions, and

3   location patterns differed across industries and country of origins.

24

This book significantly adds to this limited base of knowledge about foreign direct investment in China.

Note

1   The discussion of previous studies has drawn heavily from pp. 6-11, in Stephen Meyer and Tao Qu, 'Place-specific determinants of foreign direct investment: the geographical perspective', in M. B. Green and R. B. McNaughton (eds.), *The Location of Foreign Direct Investment*, Avebury: Aldershot, Brookfield, USA, pp.1-13.

3 The location of FDI within a subnational context

Introduction

A locational theory for foreign direct investment is obviously lacking. As discussed in the literature review, most foreign direct investment theories are devised to answer the why and how aspects of international production. The spatial dimension is mostly neglected except for Dunning's eclectic approach and Vernon's product cycle approach. Corporate geography is also inadequate in explaining the location of international business. Thus, it is imperative to construct a framework within which relevant components from location theory and from theories of foreign direct investment can be accommodated and MNE investment location choices can be systematically explored. Much of the analysis in the last chapter is reflected in the process of building the framework. Along this process, the literature review continues in a sense that relevant studies are brought in and incorporated in the framework.

In this chapter, the types of firms are discussed first, since different types of firms are related to different theories as discussed in the last chapter. Following is a brief evaluation of these different theories in their usefulness toward building our comprehensive locational framework. Then, a comprehensive locational framework is presented with a detailed discussion of each of the three dimensions.

Firm types and an evaluation of relevant theories

Three relevant types of firms exist: single-plant firms, multi-plant enterprises, and MNEs. These three types of firms represent all forms of profit seeking economic entities in the marketplace. The differences and relationships between them have important implications for putting their different locational mechanism within contexts.

Two dimensions of firms: organizational and market orientation

Among all the characteristics of firms, two basic dimensions can be identified: organizational and market orientation. Along with the spectrum of firm size from small to large, the separation of units within an enterprise both spatially and functionally can also be discerned (Lloyd and Dicken, 1977). As for the market orientation dimension, a firm can always be classified as indigenous or MNE depending on whether it operates in foreign markets beyond its domestic markets.

The cross classification of these two dimensions generates three practical categories of firms: single plant firms, national multi-plant enterprises, and MNEs. The distinctions among these different categories of firms cannot be over emphasized. They can be differentiated not only by their characteristics and locational requirements, but also by their roles in a modern economy. Moreover, they also represent the main subjects of study of different theories, with the single plant firms as the subject of study of classical location theory, multi-plant national enterprises as the geography of the corporation, and MNEs as international business. The purpose of drawing a distinction between these categories of firms is to expose the location of international business within the context of firm characteristics and of theoretical explanation.

Distinctions between MNEs and national enterprises

MNEs usually have many net advantages over indigenous firms. These advantages confer on the MNEs or their affiliates an element of distinctiveness that gives them an edge over their competitors in similar locations. These advantages, as succinctly summarized by Kindleberger (1969), Caves (1971) and Gray (1972), include:

1   better access to production technology, knowledge, and information,

2   better access to factor inputs as well as domestic and international markets,

3   distinctive enterprise-specific (ownership) advantages such as characteristics of products, and

4   economies of scale and vertical integration.

Distinctions between single plant firms and functional units of large enterprises including MNEs

The differences between single plant firms and multi-plant enterprises including MNEs are multifaceted. First, a functional unit of an MNE is an extension of an existing complex system of production, marketing, and financing from which the branch plant can draw resources. Second, a unit from an MNE usually does not have an independent identity as opposed to a single plant firm. When choosing a location, a single plant firm can pursue a sole objective, be it profit maximization or cost minimization, as assumed in classical or neoclassical location theory. On the contrary, the existence and development of a branch plant must conform with the overall strategy of MNEs. Third, the relationships of a unit with other units within an MNE may be more important than its relationships with firms in the same industrial group or within the same region.

The locational implications of the difference between a single plant firm and a branch plant of a large enterprise are twofold. First, because of its close relationships with other units within the MNE both functionally and economically, a unit from an MNE will not be evaluated by its profit or loss criteria alone. This enhances its lessened sensitivity to location specific factor costs. This means that the value of a location does not depend on its inherent advantages only. Economically speaking, the structure of factor cost encountered by the MNE in any given region is not necessary based on the local market for the factor (Vernon, 1974).

An evaluation of relevant theories

The relevancy of various theories in explaining the location of foreign direct investment within a subnational context can be evaluated within a framework formed by the unit of analysis (along with the behavioral assumptions) and the locational component in each theory. The unit of analysis refers to whether a theory deals with a single plant firm(s) or a multi-regional firm(s) or MNE(s). The locational component of a theory can range from one that has no explicit spatial component (although it may have spatial implications) to one that explicitly deals with the locational and spatial aspects of the units of analysis.

Comparing the treatment of location of two sets of theories is sufficient: international business and corporate geography. The relevancy of other theories will surface along the way of building a comprehensive conceptual framework of MNE investment locational choice.

Within international business theory, most theories do not have a spatial component except for the product cycle model and the eclectic paradigm. Even with the right unit of analysis, international business theories are aimed at explaining the phenomenon of international production, including the product cycle model and the eclectic paradigm that both have a spatial component and strong locational implications. Furthermore, the locational component in these two theories is a classical approach where emphasis is put on the relevance of special localized factors. It is shown later that locational choice is far more than the balance of the pulls of various localized factors. On the contrary, location theories, especially classical location theory, does not have the right unit of analysis although it specifically deals with the location of firms.

The comparison between international business theories and classical location theory reveals both the weakness and strengths of both within the context of studying the location choice of MNE investment. The strengths and relevancy of international business theories lie in the analysis of the nature of MNEs and the characteristics of MNE investment for both behavior and strategies. This stands in contrast with the classical location theory where the unit of analysis is single plant firms, whose

29

behavior is dictated by the market. The strength of location theory is, of course, the sole goal of understanding the location behavior of firms.

Corporate geography, rooted mainly in organization theory, the theory of the firm (including MNEs), and location theory, bridges the two extremes to a great extent. However, in its eagerness to solve every problem concerning large corporations including MNEs, it takes the whole firm as a unit of analysis and deals with various problems ranging from firm-environment relationships, spatial system and evolution, and spatial adjustment. It is inappropriate for this analysis because of the unit of analysis of the MNE investment location choice within a subnational context is the functional units within a complex organizational framework.

The inadequacy for each of three theories to deal with the locational decision of MNE investment is obvious. However, a synthesis of these theories is not sufficient to provide explanation. The dynamic nature of the location of foreign direct investment requires we draw from regional economic development theory, cumulative causation theory and, even the product cycle theory.

The location of foreign direct investment within a subnational context: a three dimensional conceptual framework

Given the sheer variety of foreign direct investment and the myriad locational factors underlying the location of foreign direct investment, searching for an all-embracing theory for the location of foreign direct investment may seem futile. Nevertheless, a conceptual and theoretical framework for a study should employ an eclectic approach and incorporate most of the valid theoretical aspects and arguments.

Building such a framework can start with the basic components of a simple MNE model (Rugman, Lecraw, and Booth, 1985, pp.99-104). Along the way, various relevant theoretical components from location theory and foreign direct investment theories can be incorporated. The simple MNE model states that an MNE as an economic entity needs to consider two sets of variables to engage in effective decision making about its global strategy. The two sets of variables are internal and environmental variables, with environmental variables consisting of country-specific or location-specific relevant factors that are exogenous to the firm. It is from these two sets of variables that an MNE's strategic and tactical planning spring.

Locational decisions should be important components in both MNEs' strategic and tactical planning. As such, with some clarification and modification, the basic structure of this simple MNE model should be transferable to our conceptual framework for the location of foreign direct investment. This locational model should depict the location of foreign direct investment within a dynamic environment and firm development process. Analogous to the MNE model, the locational model should also include two basic dimensions: firm-specific variables (FSVs) and location-specific environmental variables (LSVs).

FSVs are analogous to the company factors in the MNE model. Nevertheless, there is a difference. In the MNE model, company variables refer to the special advantages of MNEs. This is also true in Dunning's ownership specific advantage condition. In our locational model, however, this dimension is all embracing and is used to identify

30

a specific MNE. Besides firms' ownership specific advantages, foreign direct investment can also be distinguished by different home countries. Furthermore, foreign direct investment can be classified according to MNEs' global strategies and/or objectives of MNEs' tactical planning. One such example is the dichotomous classification of MNEs as either market-oriented or export-oriented MNEs. Firm size may also represent another scheme to differentiate firms involved in international production.

LSVs should include all the factors that are exogenous to a specific MNE at a point in time and that bear influence on the locational decision of that MNE. They together form the actual environment within which MNEs make their locational decisions. This environment should have two basic components. One component includes the relevant aspects of reality of a host region, which can be grouped into three categories: economic variables, noneconomic variables (political, social, and cultural variables), and governmental variables. Another component concerns the industrial structures within which MNEs make their location decisions. The presence of other MNEs in a host region may form a very important environmental variable to some MNEs.

A dynamic locational model of foreign direct investment can be completed by adding a third dimension: a temporal and dynamic dimension that captures the dynamic nature of the location process of international business. Without this temporal dimension, however, the locational model is just a static matchmaking matrix. This temporal dimension can be further exemplified in several aspects. First are the evolutionary changes in a host economy. The essence of these changes is not only shown by the magnitude of environmental variables, but also by the changes of the magnitude and nature of impact of other LSVs on the location of foreign direct investment. This is because the impact of one variable may not be exempt from the nature and importance of other variables.

Second, a firm evolves in maturity of products and organizational structure. It is well established that the strategic planning and tactical actions (including the location and allocation of resources and production) vary with the growing processes of an MNE, as do its locational variables.

Third, the most important aspect of this temporal dimension is the interaction of foreign direct investment and environmental variables, that makes this locational model a dynamic mechanism. At the beginning, within a certain period, multinational enterprises may just respond to various environmental factors, rather than determine them. Yet, the presence of a certain amount of foreign direct investment may change the social and economic reality of a host country or region. These changes will in turn exert impacts on the future inflow of foreign direct investment.

To summarize, this locational model of foreign direct investment consists of three main dimensions: firm-specific variables, locational specific variables, and a temporal dimension. Each dimension is also multifaceted. Multinational enterprises respond to environmental factors in the short run and evolve and interact with host countries or regions in the long run. This process of interaction forms the mechanism through which the changing landscape of foreign direct investment and the location and

31

allocation of a specific MNE can be understood. These three dimensions are now further elaborated.

Firm-specific variables

Industry or product related characteristics

Distinct location behavior can also derive from the differences of market and technology, as well as the differences between industries. Three meaningful classification schemes can shed light on the location behavior of an MNE investment. One scheme is the classification by technology: the intensity of labor and capital. Another is by the general locational orientation of an industry, where an industry can be either a market-oriented, resource or material-oriented, or a footloose. Yet another scheme is provided by central place theory under which industries can be differentiated from each other by their market thresholds. It is important to note that these schemes produce two types of locations: relative location and absolute location. Relative location is exemplified by large cities as opposed to small cities. Absolute locations are exemplified by specific geographical site or location.

And finally, there is the three sector classification: agricultural, manufacturing and service industries. Most empirical studies discussed in the last chapter focus on the location of manufacturing foreign direct investment. One should not be surprised to find that foreign direct investment in the service sector such as the banking industry may respond to yet another set of location factors (Dahm and Green, 1995).

Another simple, yet meaningful, classification scheme to differentiate foreign direct investment is to divide foreign direct investment into either export-oriented or market-oriented (Reuber, 1973; Dunning, 1993). This is a hybrid classification scheme that incorporates not only the technological aspects of foreign direct investment, but also the strategies embodied in these investments. Their sensitivities to production costs and other factors may be quite different. As Moxon's (1975) study shows, the tendency to invest in lesser developed countries and build offshore plants in the electronics industry is strongly related to the high labor intensity and the cost considerations resulting from import competition. This implies that export-oriented foreign direct investment is usually of standardized technology and would be geared to low labor cost regions. Dunning (1980, p. 13) also exemplifies the preferences of location specific factors by different MNEs.

While most empirical studies discussed in the last chapter focus on the location of manufacturing foreign direct investment, there is evidence that other industries in the service sector such as the banking industry may respond to a different set of LSVs (Dahm and Green, 1995).

Firm size related characteristics

The second group of FSVs are related to firm size and technology strategies. The conventional view of the ownership advantages (Vernon, 1966, 1971 and 1979;

32

Dunning, 1979 and 1980) possessed by MNEs was derived from the observation of large US MNEs predominantly operating in oligopolist industries. These firm specific advantages are usually knowledge related intangible assets derived from heavy expenditure on research and development that is a luxury almost exclusively belonging to very large MNEs. Horst (1972), Caves (1974c), and Grubaugh (1987a) confirm statistically that firms with large size and intangible assets are most likely to invest abroad and become multinationals.

Evidence from newly industrializing countries (NICs) (Chen, 1992; Yeon, 1992) suggests that the propensity for small and medium firms to invest abroad is clearly related to their growth performance. This is in contrast to the inevitable sequential development process of large innovative MNEs as depicted by Vernon's product cycle model. Moreover, the comparative advantage approach to foreign direct investment (Ozawa, 1979) might be more pertinent to explaining these firms going international. The changes in the comparative advantages forged by some macroeconomic factor wages increase and appreciation of currency between NICs and developing countries may urge firms to invest abroad to reduce costs.

Besides the production technology and firm size characteristics, the modes of entry are one aspect of firm characteristics that could affect the locational behavior of foreign direct investment. For example, joint ventures (Beamish, 1987; Beamish and Banks, 1987) often have different locational requirements than that of wholly foreign owned production. Empirical evidence as to locational determinants of different modes of entry can be found in (Green and Cromley, 1986; Cromley and Green, 1985; Green, 1985).

Country related characteristics

The third dimension of FSVs is associated with different home countries. One should not ignore that within Dunning's eclectic model the country-specific characteristics can also be referred to home countries upon which the ownership advantages of MNEs are spawned. The relationship between the two is well explained by Dunning (1979, Table 6, p. 280).

Considering the differences between developed countries and other countries including NICs in market sizes and level of economic development and a host of other factors, it is no surprise to find out there are stark contrasts between the firm characteristics of MNEs from developed countries (Dunning, 1988b, 1993; Lall, 1979; Horst, 1972) and those from developing countries. Lecraw (1977), Lall (1983), and Wells (1977, 1983) have shown that MNEs from developing countries are characterized by their low research and development expenditures. Their advantages are derived from operational characteristics such as production flexibility, smallness of scale, and labor-intensive technology. As a result, their competitive edge relies on their low-cost production rather than superior technology and other knowledge-related intangible assets or differentiated products and brand names.

The macroeconomic approach to foreign direct investment also implies the existence of country of origin induced differences in foreign direct investment. Although comparative advantages are not treated as a static configuration of resource

33

endowment anymore, rather as in a state of flux, there are still huge differences among countries' comparative advantages. This necessarily induces the conclusion that the industrial compositions of foreign direct investment from major source countries are possibly not identical. Each home country may concentrate on several industries that impart its national comparative advantages.

Because of the differences induced by different countries of origin, the dissection of foreign direct investment in different home countries might capture the diversity of foreign direct investment within one host country. In fact, the distinctive locational behavior of foreign direct investment from different source countries has been detected by some studies without solid explanations (Blackbourn, 1972; Watts, 1979 and 1980; Dicken and Lloyd, 1976; McConnell, 1983). McConnell (1983) ascribes the geographic proximity, the long history of presence, and inertia to spatial spread as the reason for the location preferences of Canadian, British, and Japanese foreign direct investment in the US, respectively. Within the context of Britain and Ireland whose spatial scales constrain the richness of location behavior of MNEs, distinction between different locational preferences of different source countries is made between the preference for less developed regions or central developed regions.

Location-specific variables of host countries/regions

Unlike the FSVs dimension, the dimension of LSVs includes variables exogenous to MNEs and forms an environment within which MNEs make their locational decision. Relevant factors in this dimension are sizeable in number and complex in nature. However, they can be grouped into two parts: (1) conventional locational factors that reflect the relevant social, economic, and political reality of a host region, and (2) the characteristics of the industrial structure of foreign investors in the host region.

Strategic and tactic locational decisions

Planning within an MNE can be classified into strategic and tactical, so can its locational decisions. Strategic planning concerns the decisions to enter foreign markets and the appropriate choice of entry mode. Tactical planning, on the other hand, deals with short-run operational decisions that involve optimization of production, marketing, and other aspects of an MNE operation subject to the overall strategies of the MNE. Correspondingly, strategic locational decisions may involve which foreign market to enter. Tactical locational decision making concerns mainly choosing a specific location within the chosen host country.

These two levels of locational decisions entail two different sets of LSVs: one set being crucial to an MNE's strategic locational decision and another on its tactical locational decision. Variables influencing an MNE's decision on which foreign market to enter can usually be identified with sovereign nations and be better labeled as 'country specific variables'. These variables have been extensively scrutinized by researchers in international business studies. On the other hand, geographers have paid more attention to the locational variables in an MNE's tactical locational decision making.

We should not expect these two sets of variables to be the same. The relationships between these two sets of variables are twofold. First, they may not share the same list of locational determinants. As reported in the literature review, market factors, barriers to trade, cost factors, political climate, incentives and disincentives toward foreign direct investment are the main factors determining the distribution of foreign direct investment among countries. Once an MNE has decided to enter one specific market (country), variables such as the political stability and barriers to international trade can be reasonably assumed away because they can be assumed to be homogeneous within a country. As such, these two variables may not be included in MNEs' tactical locational decision process, that is the locational decision making within a subnational context.

Second, some variables have a bearing on both the strategic and tactical locational decisions, but the nature and the weight of the impact they carry may be very different. The same amount of labor cost difference may mean different things in a firm's strategic and tactical locational decisions. This is especially true when one realizes that the impact of one variable may also depend on the nature and size of other variables.

As the tactical locational decision of MNEs is the major concern of this book, the LSVs will, from now on, exclusively refer to variables that are of spatial variation and exert some impact on the MNEs' locational choices within a host country. Following is an elaboration of some of the most important LSVs.

Factors of production

Economic factors such as land (including natural resources), labor, capital, and raw materials constitute a region's aggregate production function. They combine to determine the maximum production potential of a region given certain technologies. Since MNEs are conduits of capital and technology, the cost of labor, land, and availability of raw materials and resources may be relevant.

The importance of labor as a locational factor can be shown with two simple statistics: wages and salaries of workers as a proportion of production cost and the wage difference between countries and spatial variation of labor cost within one country (Dicken and Lloyd, 1990, pp.156-161). In the US, the proportion of wages and salaries of production workers accounted for one-fourth of the value added for all manufacturing industries in 1982. This percentage increases to 46 per cent if all the wages and salaries of non-production workers are also included. Despite mechanization and automation of production processes, labor cost will probably maintain the overall cost significance as a production factor. This is because mechanization and automation cause the gradual shift of labor force from blue-collar to white collar rather than eliminate labor as a fundamental production element.

The cost of labor as a locational factor is well founded in locational theory (Smith, 1981) and macroeconomic theory of foreign direct investment (Kojima, 1982). In classical location theory, labor is treated as a general factor that would divert the least

35

transportation cost location if the saving in labor is enough to offset the additional transportation cost incurred by the change of location. Obviously, the immobility of labor is assumed. Within the macroeconomic analysis of foreign direct investment, the comparative disadvantages of some industries in developed countries due to high labor cost and resource deficiency are considered the main reasons for these industries to shift production abroad. Consequently, labor cost should be one of the most important factors affecting the location of foreign direct investment, especially for labor intensive and export-oriented foreign direct investment. These industries are also industries of standardized technology and production processes.

That labor should be an important locational factor is also suggested by the international business approaches to foreign direct investment. Besides the cost of labor, the quality of labor is also important. Most international business approaches assume superior FSAs of MNEs over indigenous firms. The successful internalization of these FSAs in a foreign market demands a well trained and high quality labor force as one of the location-specific advantages. Because high quality labor is usually better paid, the MNEs that possess technological FSAs may be more prone to high labor cost regions.

There are also other aspects of labor that influence the location of foreign direct investment, e.g., unionization of labor. Unlike the cost and quality aspects of labor, the unionization of labor may only have a discouraging effect on the location of foreign direct investment. A higher degree of unionization usually induces higher cost and complacency in the labor force on improving skills.

Market factors

Market as a locational factor is also well established within locational theory and international business approaches to foreign direct investment. Most empirical analyzes also find it the most important locational determinant. In locational theory, the market as a locational factor exerts its impact just like other localized elements: the deviation of the production location from the market will incur additional transportation cost. Within the domain of international business approaches to foreign direct investment, however, the notion of the market is treated in a quite different way. First, the cost of penetrating a market is not incurred mostly by transportation cost, but rather by tariff and other non-tariff government regulations. Second, which foreign market to enter depends mostly on its current size and growth potential with reference to the MNE's overall strategic planning.

As the spatial units of this book focus on subnational levels, the importance of the market factor as a location-specific variable may depend on several factors. These factors are the sizes of regional markets, their relative geographical locations, and the trade frictions among them. Given the political and institutional fabric in China, this level of spatial unit concerning market factors is at the provincial level.

The location of a production unit entails not only where to produce, but also how much to produce and what technology to use. Given a certain technology, the size of the market is obviously the most important factor affecting the scale of production if the producer choses to serve local markets. If all of foreign direct investment is classified into market oriented and export oriented, market size should be positively related to the amount of market oriented foreign direct investment.

Established scale of production and clustering of economic activity in a host region

The scale of existing economic activity should also play an important role in the location of foreign direct investment. Most foreign direct investment theories have no direct reference to the scale and clustering of existing economic activities. The only exception is Dunning's eclectic approach, which has locational theory as one part of its components. Nevertheless, economies of agglomeration have a long tradition in locational theory. It is believed that firms, by placing production units spatially close to other activities, can benefit from positive externality resulting from this clustering of economic activities in space.

Both the scale and the structure of the clustering of economic activities in space can be important to the location of foreign direct investment. Given a region that has a strong industrial base, it is probably more attractive to foreign direct investment as since it can provide: a strong general and specific supporting and related industries through forward, backward, and horizontal linkages (including research and development activities); a pool of skilled labor; and economies of urbanization.

Agglomeration of foreign direct investment in space

Agglomeration of foreign direct investment in specific regions can be caused in several ways: sensitivity to one or more factors of production, economies of agglomeration among foreign ventures, following the leader, or simply the effect of uncertainty. Among these causes, the 'following the leader' deserves special attention because of its theoretical merit and the importance of the players that induce this effect. While the other three may apply to most foreign direct investment ventures, the following the leader applies mainly to major oligopolistic MNEs.

The 'following the leader' effect was systematically studied by Knickerbocker (1973). It was found that within an oligopolistic market environment other oligopolists tend to follow the leader and expand into the same markets to keep stability among these oligopolists. The locational consequences of this search for stability would be concentration of MNEs in geographical terms.

To understand the implication of oligopoly theory on locational theory, one must recall the interdependency of the oligopolists on each other's pricing and investment decisions. The domain of MNEs is mainly in oligopoly structured industries, at least according to the international approaches to foreign direct investment. Once the market stability is upset by the leader by establishing a local production unit in a new foreign market and thus improving its contacts with the market, other major players within the same industry may feel threatened. It is only natural for them to follow the leader to the same market to achieve a new state of stability. This is especially true for the mature oligopolies.

Geographic location and psychic and social distances from home countries

Unlike other variables discussed above, distance factors are absent from most foreign direct investment theories, except for Dunning's eclectic paradigm. Yet, empirical evidence is overwhelming in support of the relevance of the distance factor on the location of foreign direct investment. The distance can be physical, economical, cultural, and psychological (Dunning, 1979, 1980; Green, 1985; Green and Cromley, 1986; Kravis and Lipsey, 1982; Benito and Gripsrud, 1995).

For China, the relative location of a region with reference to major port cities or major industrial centers, may affect the attractiveness of a region. Geographical proximity to major port cities or industrial centers means easier and more efficient interactions between an MNE affiliate and its parent. Because of the distance factor, distinct differences in the spatial distribution of foreign direct investment may exist among coastal regions, inland regions, and peripheral regions.

The distances between home country and host regions (host-home distance factors) measured in terms of social, institutional, and language differences may also matter a great deal in the location of foreign direct investment in China. In the first place, China is a large country with varying social fabrics across regions. Second, one of the major investors in China is Hong Kong whose people share the same dialect and have close social ties with Guangdong province.

Incentives and other governmental policies

Various incentives and disincentives (including performance requirements) may form another locational factor for foreign direct investment. The unimportance of incentives as both a theoretical and empirical factor in explaining the distribution of foreign direct investment among countries is well documented (Reuber, 1973; Lim, 1983; Agarwal, 1980). Yet, this may not be necessarily true when the distribution of foreign direct investment among relatively small countries in the same geographical region is concerned (Rolfe, Ricks, Pointer, and McCarthy, 1993). As for the location of foreign direct investment within a subnational context, government policy should be assumed to be relevant when there is no evidence to the contrary.

Incentives and disincentives should always be considered together, as incentives offered by host regions are not nondiscriminatory. On the contrary, these incentives are usually accompanied by additional qualifications in terms of performance requirement, industrial sector, and technology intensity. Together, they show the active participation in the part of the host government to channel desired foreign direct investment into desired industries and areas. The overall goal of this framework is to achieve stated objectives of inducing foreign direct investment: importation and adoption of advanced technology, managerial skills, and promoting exports.

The whole package (incentives and disincentives) may represent the balance of bargaining powers between MNEs on one side and the host government on the other. It may also represent the comparative advantages and disadvantages among host countries or regions assuming there is a supplier's market for foreign direct investment. As such, the spatial variations of government policies toward foreign direct investment within a country represent a host national government's spatial economic development policy and the comparative advantages and disadvantages among regions.

LSVs as a dynamic system

Two properties of this second dimension should be noted explicitly: FSVs as a system and FSVs as a dynamic process. FSVs as a system means the interrelationships among LSVs. If all the LSVs form a dynamic system, the assessment of the attractiveness of a specific pattern of LSV should be an evaluation of the whole package rather than just one or several specific variables. With treating FSVs being a dynamic process, we can view LSVs within the context of regional transformation. As a regional economy progresses, it goes through several stages of distinct structures (Rostow, 1956, 1960; Hoffmann, 1958; Chenery, 1960, 1979, 1988; Chenery et al., 1986, Clark, 1957). As such, the differences among regions for LSVs are not just differences in the quantity of specific variables, but also differences of structures of a dynamic process.

The dynamic/temporal dimension

The location of foreign direct investment at a point in time can only be understood as a dynamic process. The dynamic aspect of our locational framework can be dissected into three components: evolutionary changes of both MNEs and LSVs, the interaction between foreign direct investment and host economy, and the experience of MNEs. With the evolutionary changes of MNEs (Vernon's product cycle model) discussed in the literature review, only the experience effect and environmental changes are elaborated below.

Experience effect and economies of scale: the uneven accumulation of foreign direct investment in space

The assertion that MNEs must have FSAs by international business approaches to foreign direct investment is justified in part by the disadvantages that MNEs must encounter when they first enter foreign markets. That is the information cost. National firms may have the general advantage of better information about their country's economic, social, and political fabric. To an MNE, this information is critical to operate properly within an unfamiliar foreign market, and the cost of getting this information may be considerable. It should also be noted that this cost is a fixed cost.

It is only logical to hypothesize further that once MNEs have acquired this information by establishing ventures in some foreign markets, they tend to choose these already familiar markets over other unfamiliar markets for their new investment and development. This 'experience effect' was empirically proven by Davidson

39

(1980) and Yu (1990). It was found that the presence of an existing venture affects the firm's next stage investment decision.

The experience effect may also exist within a subnational context. Even if the political, legal, and institutional systems are the same across one country, one can still expect uncertainty associated with different regions of varying social and economic fabric. This is especially true for a large country like China. The experience gained in one region may not be readily transferable in total to another region.

The changing investment environment

The changes in LSVs as a whole (investment environment) constitute the third dynamic aspect of our foreign direct investment location model. These changes may be induced in part by the evolutionary forces of regional development and in part by the impact of foreign direct investment on regional resource allocation and economic growth.

The local production of MNE ventures is not simply an addition to a local economy. Rather, it starts a dynamic process of interaction between MNEs and the host region. The technology and capital induced by foreign direct investment would disturb the established price equilibrium of factors of production, change the production function, and change the industrial structure in a host economy (Lall, 1978a; Caves, 1974a). These changes will finally be manifested in the overall changes of the host region's investment environment, although they cannot be easily separated from the impact of other sources.

Initial entry versus expansion and relocation

The location of foreign direct investment should be viewed as a continuing process that consists of two stages: initial entry and continuing expansion or allocation (Grubaugh, 1987b; McConnell, 1983; Dunning, 1973). The difference of objectives and determinants between these two stages incurs a distinctive spatial behavior displayed by MNEs.

After the decision of becoming multinational has been made, the search for the location of initial entry within a country is limited and mainly based on a macro-spatial framework such as states and provinces. The emphasis of the evaluation of the locational choices is placed on the potentials to realize the overall strategies of MNEs, not on the specific attributes of specific locations. Another reason is that it is easier to gather information about a higher level of region with the limited experience of MNEs in a host country.

As MNEs become more familiar with the economic environment of host countries, the locational options for continuing expansion or allocation are increased. The perception and evaluation of location choices become more sensitive to the pattern of various factors such as labor markets, resources, and other economic attributes such as research and development facilities of individual alternatives. The location search then focuses on a lower spatial framework, e.g., an urban area or economic region. Cost considerations may grow more important.

An important point is to be made at this stage: there is interdependency among the dimensions of our location model and among variables within each dimension. This is especially important for the LSVs. The impact of one variable must be related to the nature and importance of other variables. Empirically speaking, the attractiveness of regions is of a relative nature and should reflect the tradeoff among different locational factors.

Methodology and data

Cross-section and time series analysis

The conceptual and theoretical framework presented in this chapter can be summarized in the following system:

$$Y_t = f(X_t, Y_{t-1}, Z_t) \qquad (3.1)$$
$$X_t = f(Y_{t-1}, X_{t-1}) \qquad (3.2)$$
$$Y_1 = f(X_0, Z_0) \qquad (3.3)$$

where :

Y_t	represents the amount of foreign direct investment at time period t;
Y_{t-1}	represents the amount of foreign direct investment at time period of (t-1);
Y_1	represents the foreign direct investment in the first period;
X_t	represents LSVs at time period t;
X_{t-1}	represents LSVs at time period (t-1);
X_0	represents LSVs at the initial period when there is no foreign direct investment in the host economy;
Z_t	represents FSVs at time period t; and
Z_0	represents FSVs when MNEs initially entered the host economy.

Obviously this model is not readily transferable to an operational one with the same level of complexity. It is necessary, therefore, to dissect this model into two steps: first a cross-section analysis and then comparison of cross-section analyzes over time. By taking these two steps, this comprehensive model can be subjected to statistical modeling and its essence and complexity can be revealed.

The first step is a cross-section analysis of the locational response of foreign direct investment to various location-specific variables. The basic assumption underlying all of the models is the optimality by foreign investors, whatever the kinds of optimality it might be, whether it is optimal location of minimum cost, maximum profit, optimization of marketing or financing. In any case, the locations chosen by foreign investors are assumed to be within their margins of profitability (Smith, 1981).

While the first two dimensions of the model are captured by the cross-section analysis, the dynamic aspect of the model is to be incorporated in the time-series analysis. To understand the essence of the dynamic aspect in this process, one should realize the important connections between two or more cross-section analyses. First, the characteristics of foreign direct investment at different points in time are expected to be different. Second, the locational variables or locational environments at different points of time also represent the dynamic change since its previous stage. This dynamic process of change consists of two components: the change due to the interactions of the previous locational environment with the realized foreign direct investment of previous periods, and the changes due to the evolution of LSVs and the interaction among LSVs. All these dynamic changes are embedded in the locational variable and foreign direct investment data, the complexity of which cannot be easily modeled in mathematical or statistical models.

Factual variable models versus latent variable models

The location model of foreign direct investment can be expressed in two ways. One is a 'latent variable model' where the independent variables are factors derived from a set of variables by using factor analysis.[1] These factors, much less in number, are the underlying dimensions of the set of variables. Given the problem here, more than 50 urban variables can be reduced to several hypothetical variables, i.e., factors, which can account for the observed covariation among the urban variables. By using a latent variable model, we can study the location of foreign direct investment under the assumption that foreign investors respond to major dimensions of cities such as level of urbanization rather than to specific urban variables such as the labor cost in dollar amounts.

Regression models using actual urban variables as independent variables are called 'factual variable model' in this analysis. The corresponding assumption on investors' behavior is that investors choose a location for its specific actual attributes. The usage of 'a factual variable model' and 'latent variable model' is to distinguish the differences in the independent variable plus the assumptions underlying each type of model.

Aggregated and disaggregated analysis

It is obvious that foreign direct investment is anything but homogeneous. This necessarily brings out the issue of the appropriate level of aggregation of analysis. In this book, two levels of aggregation are used. At the higher level, foreign direct investment is treated as a homogeneous group as opposed to investment made by national enterprises. At the lower level, foreign direct investment is disaggregated by its country of origin or by industrial sectors.

At each level of aggregation, homogeneity is assumed. One should realize the statistical implication of this assumption. For example, at the most generalized level of analysis, foreign direct investment inflow as a whole, the impact of one specific locational variable on every dollar amount of foreign direct investment is assumed to

42

be the same. At a more disaggregated level of analysis, this homogeneity assumption of foreign direct investment is more practically justified.

The presence of foreign direct investment and the amount of foreign direct investment

Most empirical studies are aimed at establishing certain relationships between the amount of foreign direct investment inflow (dependant variable) and various other attributes (independent variables) of cities. Seldom have the relationships between cities with any amount of foreign direct investment (foreign direct investment recipient city) as opposed to cities without the presence of foreign direct investment (foreign direct investment void city) been studied. The change from zero to non-zero is not a simple change of the amount of foreign direct investment, rather it represents a categorical data change. Foreign direct investment void cities that have zero amount foreign direct investment are simply not conceived as suitable locations for foreign direct investment for the time being for whatever reasons. They represent a totally different category as opposed to those that have some foreign direct investment.

Among cities that have already secured some foreign direct investment, the variation only represents the relative attractiveness of their virtues toward foreign direct investment. The measurement level of the data is interval. The theoretical implication of the nature of this data, thus, calls for a two-step analysis. The first step is to analyze what makes a city attract any foreign direct investment at all. The second step, then, is to analyze the difference among foreign direct investment recipient cities to find out what makes a city attract more foreign direct investment than others.

Data and the unit of spatial analysis

Data

The data used in this analysis are of two basic types. One is data on foreign direct investment and another is information on the analytical spatial unit of this analysis: cities at the prefecture level. There is no single inclusive source concerning foreign direct investment in China. Different statistical yearbooks contain data of different aspects of foreign direct investment. A complete portrait of foreign direct investment necessarily calls upon all available sources of information. It is fortunate that city data is available through yearly statistics since the early 1980s. Following are the major sources of information:

1   *China Urban Statistics*, 1985 to 1994. Various social and economic statistics are compiled and the amount of yearly realized and pledged foreign direct investment in each city is also provided.

2   *China Statistical Yearbook*, 1980 to 1992, and *China Almanac of External Economic Relations and Foreign Trade*, 1985 to 1992. These two official sources, although with some overlap, provide aggregate foreign direct investment data at the provincial level. The latter is also an important source of information on laws, regulations, and special policies concerning foreign direct investment. Each *Almanac* also provides a list of selected venture contracts signed in each year, which is the only regular official source of foreign direct investment in China at the firm level. Because this list is not inclusive and is believed not to be a scientific sample, it is not used in this analysis to draw any inference.

3   *A Survey on Foreign Invested Enterprises*. This Survey, which covered the foreign invested ventures (CJVs, EJVs, WFVs) registered during 1978 to 1987, was conducted in 1988. The basic entries in this publication are the location, size (register capital), duration, venture type, products, starting date, and home country.

The unit of spatial analysis, urban core, and city periphery

This book is centered on the spatial analysis of cities at the prefecture level and above. This choice of an analytical unit reflects both data availability and the appropriateness of spatial analysis on a subnational level. Under the central government, China's administrative structure is divided into three levels: province, prefecture, and county. There were only 31 provincial administrative and spatial units in 1992. The data on this level of spatial unit are systematic. Yet, if this analysis were centered on the provincial units, the richness in the spatial variation would be sacrificed and vigorous statistical model building would be questionable. Prefectures would be an acceptable analytical unit except that it is almost impossible to collect data on prefectures. The reason is that data on prefectures are only published by each individual province. Similarly, analysis based on county level is also out of the question.

Analysis based on cities provides an alternative to this dilemma as systematic urban statistics have been made available since the early 1980s. Along with the hierarchy of political and economic autonomy, there are three levels of cities in China:

1   cities that are empowered as a province but report directly to the central government,

2   cities at prefecture level, and

3   cities at county level.

There are only three provincial level cities: Beijing, Tianjin, and Shanghai, all of which are national urban centers. Prefecture level cities include most of the provincial capitals and other major cities. The number of prefecture level cities has been increasing in the past decade. The number of county level cities is the largest.

Differences between different levels of cities are shown not only in political and administrative status, but also in their spatial structure. For a county level city, the spatial components are the many villages at the bottom of the urban hierarchy, some townships in the middle, and one bigger township at the top that is host to the city government. A prefecture level city is much larger than a county level city as it usually consists of more than two counties and/or county level cities. The city government of a prefecture level city is usually situated either at a provincial capital or a major city in both economic and demographic terms. The spatial structure of a provincial level city is not that different from a prefecture city. As they are chosen as the units of analysis, prefecture or above level cities are referred only as cities in this research to avoid unnecessary redundancy.

There are two spatial components in a city as far as the government survey is concerned: the city proper that is officially designated as urban and the counties or county level cities under its administration. A city proper usually consists of the largest built-up urban area in the city and a thin rim of agricultural suburbs surrounding the entirely built-up area. Without special note, this city proper will be referred as urban core (of a city), and the counties surrounding it as city periphery.

The analyzes in this research requires data consistency over time. Some cities are excluded from the statistical analysis because of the inconsistency in their city boundaries. Between 1984 and 1986, 100 cities were consistent in their boundaries. Between 1984 and 1991, however, this number was reduced to 87.

Conclusion

A three-dimensional location framework has been built upon existing theories and empirical studies. It includes such dimensions as FSVs, LSVs, and a third dynamic dimension. Given the complexity of the framework, a methodology is also designed to turn the framework into an operational model without losing the essence of the framework. A series of cross-section analyses can be taken to study the dynamic process. By disaggregating the first and second dimensions, we can also explore the diversity within each dimension. Both latent variable models and factual variable models are used. With different assumptions underlying these models, it will allow the comparison of the efficiency plus explanatory power of the two types of models.

All statistical model building and analysis are based on two basic data sets: a firm joint venture data set and an urban data set consisting of three years of urban statistics. The spatial unit of all analysis is the city at prefecture level or above.

Note

1   Refer to *Introduction to Factor Analysis* and *Factor Analysis: Statistical Methods and Practical Issues*, both by Jae-on Kim and Charles W. Mueller, Sage Publications: Beverly Hills, 1978.

4 The philosophy, objectives, and process of inducing foreign direct investment

Introduction

This chapter provides an overview and analysis of China's open door policy and the process of inducing foreign direct investment since 1979. As an integral part of this book, this chapter does more than just sketches out what happened during the years 1979 to 1992. First, the inducement of foreign direct investment during this period is treated as a dynamic process. Second, the inflows and locations of foreign direct investment are viewed within the context of government policy advancements and improvement of the investment environment in China. Finally, the analyses in this chapter ensure that the locational models in the following chapters are not blindfolded statistical exercises.

˙ Starting with the philosophy of China's economic development policy, the eclectic framework of China's open door policy is also discussed. As part of China's overall means to achieve the goals of its open door policy, the functions that foreign direct investments are supposed to do are different from those assigned to international trade and importation of technology. Following is the analyses of foreign direct investment processes and involvement in China during the years 1979 to 1992. The delineations of the stages in the process and the major characteristics that differentiate one stage from another are examined within the context of the advancement of China's open door policy. Finally, the macro-pattern of spatial distribution of foreign direct investment and the major sources of foreign direct investment are elaborated.

The philosophy and major components of China's Open Door Policy

Development philosophy

China's open door policy since 1979 has signified a significant change in China's pre-1978 autarchic development strategies. It was acknowledged that China's development and modernization could benefit from outside inputs, especially the technology from developed countries, even when the inputs are from totally different social and economic systems. China's policies differ from other developing countries in many distinct ways. These differences derive not only from China's ideological and political circumstances, but also from its economic circumstances.

From the vicissitudes of the nation, the Chinese have learned that a strong economy is the pillar for a nation's independence. The awareness of building a strong and independent economy has been the underpinning of ideology and economic policy since the 1949 communist party take over of mainland China. Although China had enjoyed great cultural and economic achievements before the 1880s, the very fact that modern technologies started and flourished in the West and the backwardness of the Chinese economy since the 1880s made it nearly impossible for China to be economically strong without help from the western developed countries.

However, there are many reasons for China to be wary about the presence of western influence and the possible negative impacts of depending on developed countries. China does not want to lose its independence, either political or economic, or the induction of social and political disturbances. As such, dialectically speaking, China's conscious opening to the West is only the means via which China achieves its goal-independence from the western powers. And, this process has to be achieved step by step.

Import-substitution: the cornerstone of China's eclectic Open Door Policy

The basic eclectic framework of China's open door policy, although never officially stated, consists of two basic components: import substitution and export promotion. They are the underpinnings of China's open door policies and are embedded in major laws and regulations concerning foreign direct investment. Export promotion and resource exploitation are very important in helping China's long-term import substitution development and may be even more important in the short run.

There is no doubt that China's dialectic development philosophy underlies this eclectic open door policy framework. Yet, the bearing of China's economic reality and circumstances are just as important. The importance of import substitution can be explained by two aspects of China's economic reality: the size of its market and its established economic foundation.

China has the largest population in the world, though its economy is presently of low technological quality. The abundance of its natural and agricultural resources places China in the upper tier of countries. The sheer size and abundance of resources make China a huge market, even when one considers the current level of economic development. The fundamental goal of China's development is to satisfy its own market, and not to build an economy to serve the world. If China were to succeed like Japan and some small newly-industrialized countries (NICs) did, its export volume may be well beyond the capacity of the world market. Consequently, import substitution has to be the basis of China's open door policy.

Besides its market size, China also has a stronger economic foundation than other developing countries that are starting to use or have been using foreign capital.

Consequently, the issues of development are not the inception of major industries, but the expansion of the economy, the adjustment of its economic structures, and the upgrading of the technological infrastructure. The expected role for foreign direct investment, then, is to bolster this modernization drive, along with foreign funds and direct importation of technologies and equipment. Domestic resources are and will remain central to China's development.

While the fundamental importance of import substitution is justified, this does not diminish the significance of an export promotion strategy. In fact, export promotion is an integral part of the eclectic framework. The neoclassical economic theory on the importance of trade in the development of a country is wholly embraced by China's policy makers. Increasing exports is viewed as the necessary means to expand foreign exchange earnings, which in turn, aids the inducement of advanced technologies and equipment according to the government's long term import substitution strategies.

Closely related to the export-promoting strategy is another strategy, resource exploitation, which is usually employed by some developing countries with abundant natural resources. Foreign investment and MNEs' involvements are applied to the exploitation of a host country's rich resources (including cheap labor), stimulating the export of agricultural and mineral products and labor-intensive processed products. In the end, foreign exchange earnings can be greatly facilitated.

Objectives of inducing foreign direct investment

The previous discussion of the overall strategies of China's 'open door' policy has been officially dubbed 'the policy of foreign trade and utilizing foreign capital'. This policy has been carried out via three major vehicles: trade, use of foreign capital, and importation of technology and equipment. Foreign direct investment comes under the second category that also includes foreign loans, both government and commercial. Different vehicles have been assigned different functions.[1]

The scarce foreign exchange obtained by exports has been under tight control by the government to secure the importation of advanced technology and equipment, and materials that are not available in the domestic market. Preferences have been given to upgrading an existing key technological infrastructure and the importation of technology that can boost either export or import substitution. Sectoral preference has been centered on the leading industries of the national economy. Among the avenues used, China started by acquiring complete sets of equipment and key equipment. After mid-1980, however, the importation of technology through licencing agreements began to gain currency. The percentage of dollar amounts by licensing agreement increased from 7.4 per cent in 1985 to 13.4 per cent in 1988.[2]

Foreign loans (mainly long term loans from foreign governments, the World Bank, the IMF, etc.) are important in the eyes of Chinese officials. How to bring or just keep up the 'bottleneck' sectors such as energy, transportation, and communications with the pace of economic development has been a persisting headache to China's policy makers. The long terms, low interest rates, and handsome grace periods of these loans make it justifiable to channel them into upgrading China's infrastructure.[3]

The different advantages of using this approach were clearly realized when China's open door policy was initiated. Foreign direct investment is viewed as the most efficient vehicle for getting capital, technological knowledge, and managerial skills that are much needed to bring China's economy to world standards. If a foreign investor is serious about making some profit and consequently makes a commitment in China, it may also be in his best interest to provide the knowledge and product development necessary to make the project a success. Equity joint ventures are especially favored because by working in a partnership, the Chinese stand to learn more quickly from their foreign counterparts. This preference might explain the fact that the first law concerning external economic relations was the joint venture law adopted only several months after the Third Plenum of the 11th Congress of the Communist Party held in December 1978.

Stated first in the Law of the PR China on Joint Ventures Using Chinese and Foreign Investment, the joint venture laws, which were repeated and detailed in subsequent regulations and government officials, provide the objectives of inducing foreign direct investment:

1   to absorb advanced technology and equipment to upgrade existing structures and to improve the economic efficiency of the current economic system;

2   to utilize foreign capital to boost China's economic development;

3   to gain access to foreign markets and promote exports in order to increase foreign exchange earnings; and

4   to learn and master advanced managerial skills through cooperation with foreign companies.

It should not escape one's attention that these objectives mirror the goals of China's overall open door policy. The key words are capital, technology, and export that form the basic elements of import substitution and export promotion.

This eclectic or comprehensive system of objectives set aside for inducing foreign direct investment has important implications for understanding the characteristics of foreign direct investment in China. For one thing, one can expect a sheer diversity of foreign direct investment since achieving these objectives can only be carried out by multiple players and through multiple channels. Different foreign direct investment in terms of technological intensity and export propensity and motivation and commitment can find different niches in China's development process.

Mechanisms of channeling desired foreign direct investment

It is clear that two kinds of ventures are most welcome in China: export oriented and advanced technology enterprises.[4] The former produce exports and the latter introduce advanced technology. These kinds of ventures are justified in view of China's advantages, namely the potentially huge market and abundant cheap labor. If a foreign company profits from China's low labor cost, it should not further exploit China by selling its product in China's market. If China is willing to render its market, the foreign company is expected to bring what China does not have, advanced technology and knowledge in return. As for sectoral preference, manufacturing industry and agriculture are generally encouraged and the service industry is not. Technology intensive industries such as electronics and the computer industry and communications equipment manufacturing are most welcome.

The mechanism devised to channel the desired foreign direct investment into China and achieve the stated objectives is created by hundreds of laws and regulations that affect foreign companies. These laws and regulations not only govern the legal responsibilities of a foreign company, but also regulate the relationships between foreign companies and Chinese workers, managers, and such powerful organizations as banks, customs, and ports. Among these laws many articles are interpreted by foreign investors as incentives and disincentives according to the characteristics of their own operation. In dissecting this intricate framework and analyzing the relationships of its components, regulations on foreign exchange are found to play a pivotal role.

Foreign exchange functions as a mechanism for screening out undesirable foreign capital. Chinese laws stipulate that both equity joint ventures (EJVs) and wholly foreign owned ventures (WFVs) are solely responsible for their foreign exchange balance. Clearly this would not be a problem for an export oriented enterprise. This would not exclude an advanced technology venture either. The latter's import substitution products would be sold in China with partial or total foreign currency payment with funds already allocated for imports for products not produced by the venture in China. With this government guarantee and manipulation, an advanced technology venture would have no difficulty paying the cost of semi-products purchased on international markets and repatriating its profits, at least theoretically.

However, for a venture other than the previous two types, its foreign exchange balance would affect its very existence in China. First, the project would not be easily approved. Second, even if it were approved, without enough exports to the international market or foreign currency payment guarantees from Chinese governments, repatriation of profits and payment for parts importation is doomed. In the case where imported parts are necessary for production, a venture is unlikely to be able to continue for long.

The process of foreign direct investment involvement in China

A cautious step-by-step approach was adopted in China's first decade of opening to the West. This makes it natural to analyze foreign direct investment involvement within the context of policy changes. The delineation of each stage is based not only on the volume of foreign direct investment inflow and its spatial patterns of distribution, but also on the policies or regulations promulgated. These regulations exerted considerable impact on the characteristics of the inflow of foreign investment. There are roughly four stages in the process:

1   a slow start from 1979 until 1983;

2   a short lived boom and crash during 1984 to 1986;

3   a quick recovery after 1986 and an interruption in 1989; and

4   the full-fledged increase starting in 1991.

Table 4.1 gives quantitative evidence of these four stages. One can inspect the volume of foreign direct investment inflow, the number of contracts, and firm structural changes for the three types of ventures recognized by the Chinese government.

Table 4.2 is another comprehensive table showing the spatial diffusion of foreign direct investment during the process. It shows each province's percentages of foreign direct investment committed within the province total each year. With a mere glance, one can detect the spatial spread of foreign direct investment since 1979 from Guangdong Province. There are more pattern changes revealed by the table, which are incorporated in the discussion of each separate stage. The empty cells in the table show there was no foreign direct investment in relevant provinces in specific years. This intentional design is to facilitate the visual effect of the spatial diffusion.

With the information provided in Table 4.1 and Table 4.2 and a detailed analysis of China's open door policy changes, the four stages of foreign direct investment involvement in China since 1979 are discussed in greater detail (Table 4.3, Map 2).

1979 to 1983: a cautious and slow start The initiation of this process was marked by the enactment of the July 1, 1979 Joint Venture Law, the establishment of four special economic zones (SEZs) in late 1979, and other laws and regulations on labor management, tax, registration, and foreign exchange concerning equity joint ventures. This period was characterized by a slow pace of inflow, a small amount of foreign direct investment both pledged and realized, a low profile of ventures, and a predominance of cooperative joint ventures (CJV)s. Most capital was from Hong Kong (58 per cent), the US (12 per cent), and Japan (13 per cent) and was in Guangdong province (around 80 per cent), especially the SEZs. Until the end of 1983, an estimated 1361 foreign invested ventures (FIVs) had been approved, out of which cooperative joint ventures accounted for 82.5 per cent, equity joint ventures 14 per cent, and wholly foreign owned ventures 3.5 per cent. The total amount of foreign capital pledged was more than six billion US dollars.

The small total amount of foreign direct investment and the small size joint ventures offered little toward meeting the official objectives of technology transfer and export promotion. Moreover, there were no big multinational players. This limited accomplishment in China's first four years of open door policy is understand-

Table 4.1

Number of contracts and total amount of foreign direct investment pledged each year*, 1979 to 1993, in billion US$

Year	Total amount pledged	Total no. of contracts	Number of EJVs	Number of CJVs	Number of WFVs	Number of JDPs
1979-1983	6.34	1392	190	1123	48	31
1984	2.65	1856	741	1089	26	0
1985	5.93	3073	1412	1611	46	4
1986	2.83	1498	892	582	18	6
1987	3.71	2233	1395	789	46	3
1988	5.30	5945	3909	1621	410	5
1989	5.60	5779	3659	1179	931	10
1990	6.60	7273	4091	1317	1860	5
1991	11.98	12978	8395	1778	2795	10
1992	58.12	48764	34354	5711	8692	7

* Source: *China Statistical Yearbook*, 1985, 1987, 1988, 1989, 1990, 1992, 1993, *China Statistical Press*, Beijing. *Almanac of China's Foreign Trade and Economic Relations*, 1984, 1985, 1986, 1987, 1988, 1989, 1990, 1991, 1992, 1993.

Table 4.2
Spatial dispersion of pledged foreign direct investment in China, 1979 to 1992*, in per cent

Province	1979-1982	1983	1985	1986	1987	1988	1989	1990	1991	1992
Liaoning	0.1	2.2	4.8	3	3.3	3.8	5.8	7.8	4.9	3.4
Hebei	0	0.3	0.9	0.4	1.2	3.7	1.2	1.4	1.7	2.8
Beijing	7.4	3.7	7.1	16.5	19.3	2.8	1.5	1.9	2.6	2.5
Tianjin	0.1	0.3	1.3	3.7	0.4	2.2	1.6	2.1	1.8	2.1
Shandong	0	2.8	1.9	1.9	1.2	5.2	3.4	3.7	6	6.8
Jiangsu	0	0.4	2.2	1.8	2.4	6	3.7	4.5	6.7	12.4
Shanghai	3	5.9	14.5	11.9	1.5	6.6	6.9	5.9	3.9	5
Zhejiang	0	0.9	0.9	0.9	1.8	2.3	1.6	2.1	2.9	5
Fujian	0.8	5	7.1	2.6	3.6	9.2	17.3	18.4	13.2	11
Guangdong	88.3	74	41.4	34.3	38.9	49.9	51.7	44.7	48.3	36.5
Guangxi	0.2	2.1	4.3	3.3	1.4	2.2	0.5	2	0.9	1.8

Table 4.2

Spatial dispersion of pledged foreign direct investment in China, 1979 to 1992*, in per cent

(continued)

Province	1979-1982	1983	1985	1986	1987	1988	1989	1990	1991	1992
Heilongj.	-	-	0.6	0.3	2	1.2	0.9	0.4	1	0.7
Jilin	-	0.1	0.3	0.3	0.6	0.2	0.4	0.3	0.4	0.7
Neimeng	-	0.4	0.1	0.2	0.5	0.1	0.2	0.3	0.3	0.2
Shanxi	-	-	0.1	0.2	-	0.3	0.2	0.2	0.2	0.5

* 1. Each province's percentage is out of provincial total which is the major part of the national total. The national total also includes the ministry total which is the sum of foreign direct investment that is directly involved by the ministries under the State Council. The major part of ministry total in most years was accounted by the two ministry level corporations: China Off-Shore Oil General Co. and China International Trust and Investment Corporation. The joint ventures directly participated in by the former are mainly joint exploration ventures aiming at investigating the oil resources in China's sea territory. The ventures conducted by the latter, however, cover a wide range of activities.

2. Two provinces, Qinghai and Xizang, are not included in this table. There was no investment in the latter. As for the former, the pledged foreign direct investment each year was either zero or so small that it accounted for less than 0.05 per cent of national total.

Table 4.3
Spatial distribution of foreign direct investment in China 1979 to 1992*, in US$ billion

Province	Number of ventures	Amount pledged	Amount realized	Per cent of total number	Per cent of total pledged	Per cent of total realized
Beijing	3743	3.71	2.13	4.3	3.7	7.4
Tianjin	2576	1.93	.57	2.9	1.9	2.0
Hebei	2074	2.25	.27	2.4	2.3	.9
Shanxi	513	.34	.08	.6	.3	.3
Neimeng	229	.18	.03	.3	.2	.1
Liaoning	3864	3.93	1.48	4.4	3.9	5.1
Jilin	892	.54	.15	1.0	.5	.5
Heilongj	1209	.73	.21	1.4	.7	.7
Shanghai	3263	5.94	1.94	3.7	5.9	6.7
Jiangsu	10084	8.92	2.11	11.5	8.9	7.3
Zhejiang	3694	3.65	.55	4.2	3.7	1.9
Anhui	974	.47	.13	1.1	.5	.5
Fujian	7841	10.96	2.87	8.9	11.0	9.9
Jiangxi	1234	.77	.16	1.4	.8	.6
Shandong	5849	5.46	1.60	6.7	5.4	5.5
Henan	1119	1.07	.23	1.3	1.1	.8

Table 4.3

Spatial distribution of foreign direct investment in China 1979-1992*, in US$ billion, number, per cent
(continued)

Province	Number of ventures	Amount pledged	Amount realized	Per cent of total number	Per cent of total pledged	Per cent of total realized
Hubei	1798	1.34	.36	2.1	1.3	1.2
Hunan	1104	.69	.22	1.3	.7	.8
Guangdong	30779	41.77	12.57	35.1	41.8	43.4
Guangxi	1896	1.75	.42	2.2	1.8	1.5
Sichuan	1681	1.45	.27	1.9	1.5	.9
Guizhou	309	.26	.06	.4	.3	.2
Yunnan	275	.22	.06	.3	.2	.2
Shaanxi	654	1.57	.45	.8	1.5	1.6
Gansu	89	.07	.01	.1	.1	.0
Qinghai	16	.00	.00	.0	.0	.0
Ningxia	149	.06	.00	.2	.1	.0
Xingjiang	81	.18	.54	.1	.2	.2
per cent of national total	98.6	95.1	88.3	-	-	-

* 1. This table doesn't include statistics in 1984.
2. The units for both pledged and realized amount of foreign direct investment are billion US$.
3. The number in the last row reflect the province total out of national total. Consult Table 4.2 for the explanation of the discrepancy between the two.

able only within the context of the circumstances. On the one hand, China lacked the necessary legal and institutional frameworks. There were no laws governing wholly foreign owned ventures and cooperative joint ventures. The basic Joint Venture law that consists of fifteen short articles is too vague to be a clear guidance for negotiation. Clauses in each contract had to be negotiated on a case by case basis. Also, conscious of their lack of experience and fear of making unnecessary concessions might have slowed the negotiation process. On the other hand, it is common for a foreign investor to hesitate when facing an untested market. Here, although this market has great potential, it was operated under a totally different system characterized by a propensity to shortages and an absence of a free market mechanism.

1984 to 1986: a short-lived boom Unimpressed by their accomplishments and sensing the lack of enthusiasm of foreign investors, the Chinese government made its second drive in its opening to the world. A series of events from late 1983 to 1985 induced an impressive yet short lived boom that peaked in 1985. Foreign direct investment committed in 1985 reached 5.9 billion US dollars, which was more than double of that in 1984 and close to the total between 1979 to 1983. Another important feature of this period was the increasing importance of the equity joint venture as a mode of entry by foreign investors.

This boom was initiated by the release of the Regulations for the Implementation of the Law on Joint Ventures Using Chinese and Foreign Investment on September 20, 1983. This sixteen chapter and 118 article document is an immense clarification and elaboration of the basic joint venture law. The two combined to form a sufficient legal document to govern the establishment and operation of equity joint ventures. It reflects the experience that Chinese officials had accumulated during their first four years of opening to the world.

The second component of this policy drive was the opening of fourteen coastal port cities (COCs) that were bestowed with some autonomous economic decision making power and special policies over foreign direct investment (together they are called the COC policy) (Xinhua News Agency, 1984). It showed the determination of the Chinese to seriously engage with foreign investors. Early in 1985 some of the COC policy was further extended to the two river delta regions (one is centered around Shanghai and another around Guangzhou), and one triangular area formed by Xiamen, Zhangzhou, and Quanzhou in southern Fujian Province. These regions are officially labeled as coastal open region (CORs). The special policy concerning these regions will from now on is called the COR policy. Map 2 at the beginning of this book shows the location of COCs, CORs, and SEZs.

The COC policy includes the following major components (Xinhua News Agency, 1984):

1   Decentralization of economic decision making power to COC govern-ments concerning using foreign direct investment to upgrade old or build new production projects.[5] Nonproduction projects can be approved at the

whim of local governments if they do not burden central governments on foreign exchange, export quotas, or materials scarce in China;

2   preferential treatments in (a) income tax (15 per cent) for technology advanced projects or project with more than 30 million dollars US upon the approval of the Department of Finance, (b) exemption from import duties for equipment and material for the establishment of ventures and parts and material for the production of export goods, (c) exemption of export duties and sales tax for export goods, and (d) certain portions of products of technologically advanced ventures can be sold in China; and

3   the establishment of economic and technological development zones (ETDZs) in open cities. Besides the preferential treatments ascribed to urban areas of open cities, all ventures in ETDZs can have a 15 per cent income tax status and an exemption of the 10 per cent tax on the profit expatriated out of China. The only restriction was that all ventures in ETDZs must be considered technologically advanced.

If some foreign investors were still not impressed, the signing of the investment protection treaties with fourteen Western and Asian countries and the adoption of the Patent Law of the People's Republic of China on March 12, 1984 and its enactment in 1985 did. It seemed that along with these policy advances a stable open door policy and a favorable investment environment had been created. Many investors could not resist the temptation and rushed into China that created a short-lived boom in less than two years. Even some renowned multinationals such as Volkswagen, United Tire and Rubber of Canada, and Occidental Petroleum made their move into China in this bandwagon atmosphere.

The fact that foreign investors were convinced of the determination of the Chinese government to connect with the rest of the world was only partly responsible for the boom. The main reason, however, was the decentralization of economic decision making power. Investment contracts before 1984 were carefully scrutinized by higher levels of authorities. However, with the newly acquired decision making power, the COC city governments could approve investment contracts at their discretion (below a certain scale of contracts). New investment contracts aimed at upgrading an existing technological infrastructure were encouraged by the central government. The only restriction applied to new contracts was that the central government was not to be burdened with the foreign exchange balance, export quotas, major materials, or other requirements. There was more than one reason to believe that the newly bestowed economic decision making powers to local government could only be overused, if not abused. For one thing, the evaluation of local government officials largely depended on the economic performance when they were in office. Second, government officials at various levels were already conscious of the potential benefit of foreign investment to their economies.

The optimism among foreign investors, however, was premature. While cheering the fast and positive policy changes, many investors never thought the reverse could also happen. Foreign investors still did not understand how much power that the policy makers can have and how whimsical policy changes can be under a planned economy. And, policy change does not translate into economic reality quickly in a huge and bureaucratic system. A little policy reversal in late 1985, which tightened access to imports, was nothing more than a dose of reality to remind foreign investors that the Chinese economy was nothing like what they were used to and took for granted in a free market economy. Government bureaucracy and tight control on most aspects of its economy still stayed intact. These teething problems were not going to go away quickly.

What is more important, is that a limited domestic market access denied the very motivation of those foreign investors interested only in China's market. This was even true for some ventures that were considered serious about providing their technological knowledge. Beset by various problems, especially the foreign exchange problem, some ventures found it was difficult to continue their operation. This was especially true for market oriented ventures.[6] The quality of the investment environment was seriously questioned.

Because of all this, pledged foreign investment plunged in the second half of 1985 and through 1986. Both the number of contracts and the pledged capital in 1986 was slashed by one-half compared with that of 1985. The spatial pattern of distribution of foreign direct investment in this period (started from 1985) broke away from the initial pattern. While Guangdong was still the major destination of pledged foreign direct investment, its importance was reduced a great deal. Its percentage within the national total was 41 per cent in 1985 and 34 per cent in 1986. Special attention should be paid to these two percentages, as the reduction in 1986 reveals that foreign direct investment channeled in Guangdong province was more sensitive to changes of policy and investment environment.

With Guangdong's importance declining, several other regions started gaining importance as foreign direct investment destinations. Noticeably, these regions included Shanghai and Beijing, two provincial level cities and two of the most important urban centers in China, and Liaoning Province is the most important base of China's heavy industry.

1987 to 1990: fast recovery and temporary slowdown This phase was characterized by close to three years of intensive legislation and policy change which brought China's investment environment to international standards. Foreign investors' confidence quickly recovered. The increase of foreign direct investment pledged in 1987 and 1988 was around or more than one billion US dollars, so that in 1988 the total pledged amount was close to the 1985 level.

The three-year flurry of legislation and policy change from late 1986 to 1988 can be further distinguished into two phases due to incentives of their initiation and details of policy change. From late 1986 to the end of 1987, a virtually new stratum of policy was devised and carried out to improve the investment in response to the sizable fall of foreign direct investment inflow started in late 1985. Policy changes in 1988, however, resulted from China's attempt to articulate the overall strategies for economic development for coastal regions[7] which encouraged coastal regions in China to pursue an all out export-led growth strategy.

There was a large amount of legislation devised and implemented by both the central and local governments during late 1986 and early 1988 in an attempt to bring China's investment environment to international standards. Among these were the law on the wholly foreign owned ventures promulgated April 12, 1986 and the law on the contractual joint ventures passed April 14, 1988. The center piece of legislation amid this flurry of regulatory activity was the State Council's Provisions to Encourage Foreign Investment issued in October 11, 1986. Various implementing regulations were promulgated in 1987, which explained how foreign invested ventures were to deal with issues involving labor, RMB loans, customs procedures, and import and export licences.

Measures taken to improve the investment environment were divided into two sets: one was directed to all foreign invested firms as a whole, and the other directed to special types of firms preferred by the Chinese government: the export-oriented ventures (EOVs) and the advanced technology ventures (ATVs). Measures that applied to all foreign invested ventures (FIVs) included autonomy of labor management (mobility and wage) and operation, reduction of excessive costs levied by local governments, reduction of customs duties and consolidated taxes, and more important, allowing foreign exchange swaps.

Foreign investors, especially those aiming at China's market, had been having trouble balancing their foreign exchange. The joint venture law stipulates that FIVs should be ultimately responsible for their own foreign exchange balance. For ventures that can produce internationally competitive products and import substituting goods, their products may be sold in China and be partially paid for with hard currencies. As foreign reserves were tightly controlled by the central government, this arrangement made market-oriented ventures vulnerable to the fluctuation of government policy on foreign reserve.

Foreign exchange problems were compounded when the sourcing of material and semi-products as inputs in China did not turn out as originally expected. Because of more material sourcing in international markets, production costs increased and joint ventures would probably lose their competitive edge in both international markets and China. To relieve the foreign exchange problem, the provisions allow joint ventures to swap their Renminbi (the Chinese currency, which literally means 'the people's currency' and can be abbreviated as RMB) earnings for foreign currencies among themselves under proper government supervision.

An earlier government regulation, the State Council's Provisions on Foreign Exchange Balancing in Sino-Foreign Joint Ventures, also provided other options. One option is designed specifically for joint ventures that are to bring advanced technology to China and/or produce import-substituted products. These ventures should specify the portion of their products to be sold in China in their contracts. Based on the information specified in the contracts, governments will then include the purchasing of the stipulated portion of products in their foreign exchange usage plan. Another option is to allow joint ventures to sell their products to firms in SEZs or ETDZs of coastal open cities for foreign exchange rather than RMB. Upon approval, products can also be sold to firms that are outside these regions and with foreign exchange ability. The third alternative for a joint venture to balance its foreign exchange is to export Chinese products using their RMB earnings. In fact, this procedure may not be an effective way because of the difficulty of obtaining a license and because the intended exports will most probably take China's export quotas. Finally, if a foreign investor has more than one joint venture in China, he can balance the foreign exchange problem among his own joint ventures.

Apart from those measures that could be applied to all FIVs, more preferential treatment was given to ATVs and EOVs. First, income tax rates were reduced to as low as 10 per cent and these two types of firms are exempt from profit remittance tax. Second, land use fees were reduced. Other basic utility fees (water, electricity, transportation and communication services) were charged at the same level as for local state-owned enterprises. And, these two types of firms have priority on basic infrastructure and services. Third, ATVs and EOVs have priority to obtain loans upon the approval of the Bank of China. Finally, they are exempt from labor subsidies beyond labor insurance, welfare costs, and housing subsidies, which reduces labor cost a great deal. Undoubtfully, all these measures have put ATVs and EOVs in a more advantageous position than most indigenous enterprises.

This center piece of legislation itself made a major change in China's investment environment. And its impact was greatly magnified by an immediately following frenzy of local legislative activities. It is virtually impossible to detail the contents of local special policy toward foreign direct investment because of the sheer amount of legislation. However, it is fair to say that more concessions were made in land use fees, income taxes, custom duties, and labor costs. Some of these concessions might not have been necessary except for the competition among regions.

Taking into account all the policy changes since 1979, China was then considered to have aligned its investment environment with international standards. (US-China Business Council, 1988). Most of the distortions of the pre-1978 Chinese economy had been removed. The remaining problems facing foreign investors would arise from the nature of the Chinese economy rather than being specific to joint ventures.

The accompanying changes concerning foreign direct investment with China's new coastal economic development strategy in 1988 were multifaceted. First, Hainan was elevated to provincial status and the whole province was declared a SEZ. COC policy was further extended to Shandong and Liaoning Peninsular and the coastal regions of Hebei and Guangxi provinces. In addition, more tax concessions were made. Second, Guangdong, Fujian, and Hainan provinces, as regions for comprehensive reform experiments, were conferred more autonomous power to transform their economies into export-led ones. Third, a second round of national and local legislative efforts followed. Fourth, new zones such as 'high and new technology development zone,' 'tax haven,' and 'investment zones for Taiwan investors' within SEZs, COCs and CORs were created.

Apart from the recovery of the total amount of foreign direct investment pledged, there are other characteristics that mark the distinctness of this period. One was that equity joint ventures surpassed cooperative joint ventures as the major investment form by foreign investors in 1985. This result was no doubt encouraged by the

Chinese government's preference on equity joint ventures. No preferential treatment was extended to cooperative joint ventures in 1984. Even the legal status of cooperative joint ventures was only explained in 1988, almost eight years after China's opening to the world. Another characteristic of this period was the surging importance of wholly foreign owned ventures after the enactment of the 1986 Law on Wholly Foreign-Owned Enterprises. It surpassed cooperative joint venture as a form of entry by foreign investors in 1989 (by pledged amount) and 1990 by total number of contracts.

The spatial distribution of this period also distinguishes itself from the previous ones. The fact that more regions have preferential treatment toward foreign direct investment encourages the spatial diffusion of foreign direct investment. After 1987, foreign direct investment in China was no longer concentrated in several provinces and cities, i.e., Guangdong, Beijing, and Shanghai. Rather, most coastal provinces became seriously engaged in inducing foreign direct investment, especially such coastal provinces as Jiangsu, Shandong, Liaoning, and Fujian. The first three happened to be and still are among the most important provinces in China in both economic and demographic terms. As Fujian Province shares much in common with Guangdong Province, such as being geographically and socially close to Hong Kong and overseas Chinese, it started to become an important destination of foreign direct investment second only to Guangdong Province. During the period from 1988 to 1990, while Guangdong Province held 45 per cent to more than 50 per cent of total foreign direct investment in China, Fujian Province's share was nine to 19 per cent.

The protest by western countries after the 1989 incident was nothing more than a temporary delay for the inevitable: a full-fledged inflow of foreign direct investment into China. While the amount of foreign direct investment pledged in 1989 was virtually the same as that in 1988, there was actually an increase of one billion US dollars in 1990. All of this foreboded what was to come in 1991.

1991 to 1992: the start of the inevitable soaring increase A new phase started in 1991 that brought both the opening of China and the involvement of foreign investors to a point of no return. The yearly increase of foreign direct investment pledged in 1991 alone was more than 5 billion US dollars. The total, 12 billion US dollars, was twice the total of the early booming year of 1985. Any doubt on the start of a new phase, if there was any, had been erased by the astonishing 46 billion dollar increase in 1992.

This new phase did not come without nurturing in terms of policy changes by the Chinese government after the '1989 Tiananmen Square Incident.' To the outside world, the Chinese government initiated a series of policy changes to salvage the loss of confidence because of the incident. To the Chinese government, however, it was just another step in its long term open door policy. The major policy advances in this period were:

1   the opening of tax-free zone,[8]

2   allowing foreign investors in land development,

3   promoting high and new technology industry development zones (HTDZs)[9] in major provincial capitals,

4   revisions of joint venture laws,

5   detailed regulations on implementing the wholly foreign owned venture law, and

6   measures taken to speed the development in Shanghai to regain its status as one of the most important cities in the Far East.

The major changes in the revision of joint venture law were the official time-limits set up for official approval within three months and that manufacturing joint ventures are no longer required to include in their contracts the duration of the ventures.

With the full-fledged increase of foreign direct investment inflow, the structure of spatial distribution also changed. First, Guangdong Province became less important as a destination for the foreign direct investment inflow. It accounts for only a little more than 36.5 per cent of national total in 1992, close to its record low of 34 per cent registered in 1986. Second, 50 per cent of the national total in 1992 was more evenly distributed among the ten other coastal provinces or provincial level cities, with only Fujian and Jiangsu Province registering a little more than 10 per cent of the national total. Third, several inland provinces started to attract considerable amounts of foreign direct investment, especially Sichuan, Hubei, Henan, and Jiangxi Provinces.

The spatial variation of China's Open Door Policy

One can easily see from the last section that the post-1978 open door policies have not been spread evenly across China. Experiments with a specific policy in a special regional entity or several cities and regions before generalizing it to the whole country have been a recurring feature. This was not done without reasons. It actually reflects the Chinese government's cautiousness in converting its central planning economic system to a 'socialist market economy'. A decade's worth of economic reform toward 'socialist market economy' did not reshape China's whole economic system, which was especially true in the early 1980s. The economic reform in the forms of ownership reform, expansion of policy making power of enterprises, introduction of a market mechanism into the pricing of industrial and agricultural products, and greater automatic power to provincial governments has greatly changed the operation of China's economic system. Nevertheless, China remains a planned economy. The very presence of MNEs in China will induce the encounter of two different systems. To contain the consequences, learn from the interaction of the two systems, and avoid possible negative consequences before introducing changes to the whole country, some regional entities with special experimental policies were deemed necessary and created from time to time.

The spatial variation of the open door policy also reflects China's official philosophical roots in growth pole theory on the expansion of regional economic growth and conforms with its overall locational aspect of economic development strategy. Its creation was a combined effort by different levels of governments. It is virtually impossible to detail policy differences from one city or one province to another. Because of this, only the major aspects of policy variation created by the central government are discussed here. Most, if not all, of the national special policies toward foreign direct investment were granted to cities and regions in coastal provinces. Within costal provinces, cities can be grouped into three types according to the special policy and decision making power conferred to them by the central governments: SEZs, COCs, CORs, and those without special policy in the coastal provinces as the rest of the cities in inland and remote provinces (refer to Map 2).

There are five SEZs, of which four were created at the inception of China's open door policy and joined by another one in 1985, the whole Hainan Island which in 1988 was elevated to a province. Fourteen coastal open cities (COCs) were created in 1984. While COC policy mainly applies to the urban district of these cities, some SEZ policy was applied to the economic and technology development zones (ETDZs) newly created within these cities. Coastal Open Regions (CORs) were initially started at two river delta regions (the Yangtze and Pearl River Delta Region) and a triangular area centered around Xiamen, and a SEZ in Fujian Province. The COR policy was granted to more cities in during the period 1985 to 1987 and all COCs virtually formed a belt around China's coast. The spatial relationship of these three types of cities can be summarized as city points of SEZs and COCs scattered on the belt formed by COR cities.

The differential treatment of foreign investors is reflected in many aspects. Most important, these include income tax exemptions and reductions, other tax concessions on the sales tax, on the industrial and commercial consolidated tax (ICCT), on land use fees and on various service fees plus labor costs. While it is impossible and unnecessary to detail the differences, it is sufficient to state that a spectrum of special treatments was formed starting from SEZs, as the most liberal, to COCs to CORs.

Sources of foreign direct investment and importance of home countries

Out of all the countries that have private investment in China, Hong Kong, the United States, and Japan have been the three most important investors in value contribution. Hong Kong accounted for 64.3 per cent of the total amount (112.5 billion US dollars) of foreign direct investment pledged during 1979 to1992. The US and Japan trail behind Hong Kong with 7.5 per cent and 5.5 per cent, respectively. Separate statistics on foreign direct investment from Taiwan in official statistics only started in 1992. Yet, one year's commitment alone put Taiwan as the fourth most important investor in the amount pledged. Beyond these four sources, Singapore comes next and takes 1.7 per cent of the national total. Three other developed countries, Germany, Britain, and France are farther behind with each taking around one per cent of the national total.

The relative importance of the countries also changes over time. As shown in Table 4.4, in most of the fourteen-year period, Hong Kong contributed around 60 per cent of total foreign direct investment pledged. An increase to 71 per cent in 1992 (a national total increase of 58 billion US dollars) alone brings its total average to more than 64 per cent. On the contrary, the relative importance of the US was much more impressive in the earlier stages than in later stages. While Singapore's contribution was fairly stable during these years, the importance of Germany and Britain and other developed countries fluctuated from year to year.

The value contribution by no means represents the real contribution made by each home country. By real contribution, is meant the contribution in technology transferred to China, the training brought to the workers and management staff, exports created, and the spillover effects brought to local economies. For example, although Germany's dollar amount contribution was not that all impressive, several equity joint ventures like Volgsvolgen in Shanghai have been much appreciated. This project, with much government support in many ways, initiated and has been leading the process of building a modern car industry base in Shanghai. As such, in the sense of real contribution, the role played by developed countries is irreplaceable.

Table 4.4

Changes of the relative importance of foreign direct investment sources, per cent of national total of foreign direct investment pledged

Year	Hong Kong	US	Japan	Singapore	Germany	Britain
1979-1983	58.0	11.5	12.8	0.7	0.5	4.3
1983	33.5	24.9	4.9	0.9	0.0	15.9
1985	65.3	18.2	7.4	1.2	0.3	0.7
1986	51.1	18.6	7.4	4.9	1.5	1.5
1987	53.2	9.2	8.1	1.9	3.6	0.7
1988	67.6	7.0	5.2	2.6	0.9	0.8
1989	57.9	11.4	7.8	2.0	2.7	0.6
1990	59.8	5.4	6.9	1.6	0.7	1.8
1991	62.3	4.6	6.8	1.3	4.7	1.1
1992	71.5	5.4	3.7	1.7	0.2	0.5

Another note on the contribution of different home countries is in order. The percentage of Hong Kong foreign direct investment may have been inflated, especially in earlier years. Some investment must have originated from Taiwan as the government regulations in Taiwan prevented direct investment in the mainland. As a result, if it were not for the Taiwan government's position, the value contribution of Taiwan will be much larger than was reflected in the percentage. Obviously, this will bring Hong Kong's percentage down. However, it is not possible to deny Hong Kong's prominent position.

The relative importance of each home country can be understood within the context of their respective global distribution patterns of outward foreign direct investment. For example, developed countries have been the major destinations of most of US outward foreign direct investment (Dunning, 1993, p. 23). On the contrary, outward foreign direct investment from developing countries and NICs, especially that from Singapore, has been mainly concentrated in developing countries, especially South and East Asia. A reason for that is the ability of foreign direct investment from Hong Kong and Taiwan to compete with US outward investment in Asia, as the former enjoys much greater familiarity with the business environment and social understanding with the society and compatible management style (Chen, 1983; Schive and Hsue, 1985).

As for the trend, it is possible that Hong Kong's and developed countries' relative importance will decline when South Korea and Taiwan fully take advantage of the opportunities provided by China's opening to the world.

Notes

1   'Excerpt of the Sixth Five-Year Plan of Social and Economic Development of PR China (1981-1985)', in the *Almanac (the Almanac of China's Foreign Economic Relations and Trade)* 1983, pp.11-13, Hong Kong: China Resources Advertising Co. Ltd, 1983. 2. 'Excerpt of the Sixth Five-Year Plan of Social and Economic Development of PR China (1986-90)', in *1987 Almanac of China's Foreign Economic Relations and Trade*, Hong Kong: China Resources Advertising Co. Ltd, 1987. 3. 'Excerpt of suggestions from the Central Committee of C.P. concerning the seventh five-year plan of social and economic development', in the *1986 Almanac of China's Foreign Economic Relations and Trade,* pp. 3-11, Hong Kong: China Resources Advertising Co. Ltd, 1986.

2   see, The great success in the importation of technology in 1985, pp.41-43; A brief account on the importation of technology in 1988, pp.49-50, *The Almanac* (in Chinese)

3   pp.43-45, 1987; pp 47-48, 1988; pp 42-43, 1989; *The Almanac* (in Chinese)

4   These two types of ventures were not officially defined until 1987 when much more preferential treatment was going to be conveyed to these enterprises. Export oriented enterprises were defined as export product manufacturing ventures that export more than 50 per cent by the NICs by

adopting an export-led growth strategy. Favorable international economic and political environment made such an export-led policy feasible. It was perceived that another worldwide shift of labor intensive industries had begun. The shift of labor intensive industries from the US and Japan in the mid-1960s resulted in the economic miracle of NICs. Started in the late 1970s and early 1980s, the economic transformation and macroeconomic factors led another transfer of labor intensive industries from these NICs to other developing countries in Asia. Also, coastal regions hold considerable competitive advantages compared with inland regions as well as other developing countries in labor resources, economic establishment infrastructure, and investment environment.

Considering all these aspects, an export-led growth strategy was adopted as the new economic development creed for coastal regions. The main components include: 1) encouraging the development of export-oriented labor intensive and labor and technology intensive industries based on local resources, including construction material industry; 2) actively promoting the development of industries whose markets and inputs are both based on international markets; 3) major coastal cities with an advanced technological infrastructure should take the responsibility to lead China's industrial technological development. Effort should also be made to promote export of manufactured products that have more technology content; and 4) encourage the trickle-down or spread of technology and information from coastal regions to inland regions.

Refer to 1) 'Zhao Ziyang On the Strategies for Economic Development in Coastal Regions', in the *1988 Almanac*, pp.27-32. It was an address by Zhao Ziyang, then General Secretary of Chinese Communist Party, after his two trips to coastal regions during the last two months of 1987, 2) 'Government Work Report (excerpt)', an address by then acting Premier Li Peng to the first meeting of the 7th National People's Congress, in the *1989 Almanac*, pp.1-9, 3) 'Excerpt of Vice Premier Tian Jiyun's Address to the Working Conference on the Opening of Coastal Regions', March 8, 1988, in the *1989 Almanac*, pp.15-9. 4) 'Excerpt of Comrade Gu Mu's Address to the Working Conference on the Opening of Coastal Regions', March 4, 1988, in the *1989 Almanac*, pp.25, 32.

8   Tax-free zones started in 1990 in Shanghai, and Tianjin and Shenzhen in May 1991, and Shenzhen, Dalian, and Guangzhou in 1992 June. Within these zones, ventures are supposed to produce solely for export. Starting in May 1990, foreigners were for the first time allowed to engage in the development and operation of land in SEZs, COCs, and CORs. The objectives were to speed up construction of an infrastructure and improve the investment environment. The only restriction, though, is that ventures engaging in the land development have no control over postal and communication services.

9   The experiment started in 1988 at Beijing's Haidian District where several major universities are found. Afterwards, most provinces set up their own

experiment zones in their provincial capitals. On March 6, 1991, in accordance with the 'Torch Plan' in China's 8th five year plan, State Council selected 21 such zones and recognized them as national HTDZs. The objectives of setting up HTDZs are 1) to ease the commercialization of new and high technology and the formation of new industries based on these technologies, 2) to upgrade conventional industries and improve productivity, and 3) to help the progressive transformation of regional economies. In other words, the objectives are to improve the competitive advantages of the Chinese economy.

The criteria for setting up ventures in HTDZs are 1) 30 per cent of the employees are technicians with at least a bachelor degree in their fields, 2) research and development expenditures exceed 3 per cent of total revenue, 3) 50 per cent of its total revenue must come from the sale of the products of certain high or new technologies, 4) the technology of the venture must be within eleven fields identified by the Stte Science and Technology Commission. These eleven fields include: microelectronics science and information technology, space science and space aviation technology.

Preferential treatments include 1) import and export, and 'tax havens,' 2) bank loan and other production factors, 3) import protection in case of competition from imports, 4) autonomous pricing, and 5) two year tax holiday, and tax rates of 15 per cent and 10 per cent for those exporting 70 per cent of their products.

Refer to 1) March 6, 1991, *Circular of the State Council on the Ratification of the Establishment of National High and Technology Development Zones and Related Policy and Regulations.* 2) March, 1991, *Criteria for and Identification of High and New Technology Ventures in National High and New Technology Development Zones, State Science and Technology Commission.* 3) March 1991, *Some Temporary Policy Concerning National High and New Technological Industry Development Zones,* State Science and Technology Commission. 4) March 1991, *Tax Policy Concerning National High and New Technological Industry Development Zones,* State Taxation Bureau.

5 Why these cities and not those?

Introduction

In the methodology section of chapter four, a distinction is made between the implications of the presence of foreign direct investment and that of the amount of foreign direct investment. While spatial variation of foreign direct investment commitment is examined in the next two chapters, this chapter focuses on studying the spatial mechanism of foreign direct investment commitment. The key question is what makes foreign investors choose some cities over others as the locations for their intended production. One cannot expect that the criteria of being a foreign direct investment recipient city are static. Therefore the question of how the likelihood of investment changes over time should also be answered.

The above objectives are achieved through a three-step analysis. The first is to find out what impacts several sets of dummy variables (policy, distance from the coast, distance from home countries) have on a city's likelihood of being a recipient city. In the second step, discriminant analysis is applied to uncover the impact of other interval measurement level variables. The separation of these two types of variables is of statistical necessity. The third step is to study the changes of the mechanism from one year to another.

Location specific variables included in model building

Before going into detailed analysis, the location specific variables (LSV)s for most analyses are introduced. The selection of these variables is guided by the conceptual and theoretical frameworks presented in previous chapters and is decided by the constraints of Chinese urban statistical data. The following is a list of the variable name abbreviations with explanations of what they represent:

AMOUTPUT   gross output value of agriculture and manufacturing industry, in RMB¥(0000s)

71

AVEPIPE	the length of urban underground sewage pipes per capita, in kilometers
AVERETAIL	total retail value per capita, in RMB¥(0000s)
AVEWOKOUT	productivity of labor measured in net manufacturing output per worker (state-owned and collectively owned enterprises), in RMB¥(0000s)
COCPOLICY	dummy variable designated for coastal open cities (COC)s
CORPOLICY	dummy variable designated for coastal open regions (COR)s
DCCOAST	dummy variable designated for cities other than a coastal port city but are still within a coastal province
DCINLAND	dummy variable designated for cities in inland provinces that include all the provinces other than coastal provinces and Neimeng, Xinjiang, Qinghai, Xizang, Yunnan, and Guizhou Provinces
DCPORT	dummy variable designated for coastal port cities
DSADJACEN	dummy variable designated for cities in Guangdong Province where distance from source country is in 'adjacent' category, which means a city is both socially and geographically next to at least one of the source countries
DSCLOSE	dummy variable designated for cities in Fujian Province where the distance from source country is in a category in which a city is both socially and geographically very close, although to a lesser degree than cities adjacent, to at least one home country
GAP	inequity of development between the urban area and the periphery of a city, which is expressed as the ratio of the gross manufacturing output per capita in urban area to the average of the city
KLRATIO	capital labor ratio measured in net fixed capital per worker, in RMB¥(0000s)

MP84, MP86, MP91	market potential of cities using 1984, 1986, 1991 urban statistics
MP[1]	market potential of a city
NCENTER	dummy variable designated for national urban and economic centers such as Beijing and Shanghai.
OUTPUT	total gross output value of manufacturing industry, in RMB¥(0000s)
OUTPUT%	percentage of total gross output value of manufacturing industry within the total gross output value of agriculture and manufacturing industry, in RMB¥(0000s)
RATEOUT	growth rate of gross output value in manufacturing industry, in per cent
RATEPIPE	growth rate of the length of urban underground sewage pipes, in per cent
RATERETL	growth rate of the total retail value, in per cent
RCNETER	dummy variable designated for regional major industrial and urban centers (based on urban population size and size of manufacturing industry)
RESIDOUT%	percentage of gross manufacturing output value produced by enterprises other than state and collectively owned enterprises
RETAILVAL	total retail value of a city, RMB¥(0000s)
SEZPOLICY	dummy variable designated for special economic zones (SEZ)s
TAXWELL	tax and profit ability of a local economy measured by the proportion of gross manufacturing output value submitted as tax and profit to the state, in per cent
URBANPOP	the number of people living in an urban area that is officially designated as urban
URBANPOP%	percentage of people living in the urban area within the total population of a city

VALADD%	percentage of value added in manufacturing industry within the total gross output value
WAGE	labor cost measured by annual wage per worker in state and collectively owned enterprises in urban area, in RMB¥(0000s).

All these variables can be divided into two groups. One group includes those variables such as retail value and retail value per capita measured on at least an interval scale. Another group consists of dummy variables reflecting such aspects as location, policy, or social and physical distance from home country. According to the theoretical basis of each variable, they can be grouped in the following fashion. A brief description of these groups of variables provides a basic background in explaining the statistical location models.

City size variables

Four variables can be related to the size of a city. They are URBANPOP, RETAIL, OUTPUT, and MP, which reflect city size based on population, retail markets, scale of manufacturing activity, and market potential. While other variables are self-explanatory, market potential deserves further explanation. As a calculated index, it represents both the market size and relative geographical location of the province in which a city is situated. It is assumed that the spatial friction effect does make a difference. It is also assumed that each province forms a homogeneous market compared with other provinces. All the provinces together represent the segmentation of the national market. A city can hardly form a separate market because it is geographically too small and a city government does not have the power to impose barriers between its market and others. A province, on the other hand, is different on both accounts. It follows that, for a market-oriented venture, the best location should be combination of both the size of the local market (a city market) and its ease of access to other local markets.

While each of the four variables is mainly indicative of the size of a city, they do have different foci. Also both URBANPOP and OUTPUT reflect the size of a city in absolute terms, that is, it reflects the scale of population or economic activity in a location. RETAILVAL and MP, on the other hand, are measures of a relative nature in that they are also accounted for by the consumption level in a city.

Urbanization and infrastructure Urbanization in a city is captured by URBANPOP%, the percentage of population living in the urban district. AVEPIPE, the length of underground pipes per capita in urban area, is used as a surrogate for the level of the infrastructure in the urban area. RATEPIPE is used to measure the improvement of the urban infrastructure. Accompanying the urbanization variables is OUTPUT%. It depicts the level of industrialization that is usually the driving force during urbanization, at least in the Chinese experience.

Labor variables WAGE, the average wage of workers in state or collectively owned sectors in the urban area rather than the average wage of the whole city, is used to reflect labor cost across cities. This selection is based on two reasons. First, it is generally accepted that foreign investors prefer a skilled work force that is usually available in the urban area of a city. This also means that the labor pool for foreign investors is the very same as the one that is already employed by indigenous firms, especially state and collectively owned firms. Second, labor mobility from rural areas to urban areas is low due to both strict government regulation and a poor urban housing market.

Other aspects concerning labor as a factor of production include AVEWOKOUT and KLRATIO. While the former reflects the productivity of workers, the latter (capital labor ratio) shows how well a city's workers are equipped. Given the importance of modern technology in economic growth, these two aspects combined provide an aggregate picture how a city is equipped with modern technology and equipment and how experienced and productive is its labor force.

Economic and social development variables The size of a city's economy and the level of industrialization are not the only aspects of an economy that may be relevant to foreign investors. First, there is RESIDOUT%, the proportion of economic sectors other than the state or collectively owned in manufacturing industries. China as a nation is still a predominantly state and collectively owned economy. Yet, since the economic reform and open door policy was initiated, the development of other sectors in some provinces and cities has become the dynamic force of local economic growth. Also, the bigger this percentage a city has, the closer its market mechanism resembles a free market to which most foreign investors are accustomed.

Second, VALADD% is used to reflect the depth of processing in manufacturing industries and the technology content in an economy. The third variable is TAXWELL, the ability to generate tax and profit. The stronger this ability, the stronger the financial strength a local government. The implication of this strength may be a greater effort by a local government to improve the infrastructure. The fourth variable is the rate of economic growth (RATEOUT) which reflects a city's dynamics. Foreign investors may be more attracted to growing regions than to those stagnating. Moreover, AVERETAIL, RETAILVAL and GAP are also included to reflect the level of social and economic development of cities.

Policy and distance variables The spatial variation of the Open Door Policy was discussed in Chapter Four. To capture the impact of policy instruments on the location or presence of foreign direct investment, three indicator variables are devised to represent cities with different special policies: SEZPOLICY, COCPOLICY, and CORPOLICY.

Distance, both physical and social, from one or more home countries is represented by two indicator variables: DSADJACEN and DSCLOSE. As far as this type of distance is concerned, cities in Guangdong and Fujian provinces stand out in stark contrast with the rest of the cities in other provinces. DSADJACEN represents cities in Guangdong Province that are geographically next to Hong Kong, the most important source of foreign direct investment in China. Also, people in Guangdong share close social ties with people in Hong Kong, Macau and overseas Chinese. This is due to intertwining historical, demographical, and language reasons. As a result, the social distance between Guangdong, as a location for foreign direct investment, and Hong Kong, Macau, Taiwan, and overseas Chinese as foreign investors is the least. This puts cities in Guangdong Province in a more advantageous position as possible locations of foreign direct investment. In fact, an important, if not the dominant, element in choosing the first four SEZs was the strong social ties shared between these places and overseas Chinese and their geographical proximity to Hong Kong and Macau.

Much of what has just been said about Guangdong Province applies to Fujian Province. The difference is that Fujian Province's closeness, both physically and socially, to Hong Kong, Macau, and overseas Chinese is less intensive than that of Guangdong. For example, from the point of view of Hong Kong investors, the direct link and easy access through land between Hong Kong and Guangdong Province, especially to those cities directly adjacent to Hong Kong in the Pearl River Delta region, make these cities the ideal location for their investment. The geographical proximity allows easy interaction and cooperation between investors from Hong Kong on one side and local ventures in Guangdong province on the other side. This consideration leads to the usage of another indicator variable, DSCLOSE, to label the cities in Fujian Province.

Location variables affecting the ease of interaction between home and host cities Cities are also classified into four groups by four distance (distance from the coast) variables: DCPORT, DCCOAST, DCINLAND, DCREMOTE. The consideration of these location variables is in part to simulate the effect of distance from home countries. The proximity between cities and some major sources of foreign direct investment (Hong Kong, Japan, and Taiwan and Korea in recent years) decreases in the sequence of port city, coastal city, inland city, and cities in remote provinces. The second reason is that the effectiveness of transportation and communication networks with international markets also recedes in that sequence. The ease of interaction with home countries plus international markets is assumed to matter to foreign investors. It may not just be a matter of import and export of materials and products, but also a matter of management interaction of ventures in China with parent companies in home countries. Third, the fact that most of China's major manufacturing and urban centers cluster in coastal provinces makes cities in those provinces (including port cities) more likely to receive the trickle-down or spread effect (Hirschman, 1958; North, 1955) disseminated from large centers. In brief, port cities and cities in coastal provinces overall have an advantageous position in receiving foreign direct investment plus information, technology, and the impetus of economic growth from major urban and manufacturing centers.

Variables of positions in urban system Probably not captured by all of the above variables are the effects of a city as a national or metropolitan center in terms of both its political and economic clout and many other aspects such as commerce, science and technology, and education. The three provincial level cities directly under central government control, Beijing, Shanghai, and Tianjin, are undoubtedly three national centers in many ways. The advantages of placing a venture in these cities may also include many important intangible aspects such as easier access to central decision making bodies, a more stable investment environment, and therefore less risk.

The second level of cities under this hierarchy are the major industrial centers that are also the seats of some provincial governments. The advantages that these cities possess are analogous to the three national centers, only on a regional scale. The national importance of many industrial sectors in these cities and their geographical locations make them centers second only to the three national centers. To capture the impact of a city either as a national center or a regional center, two dummy variables are included in the statistical analysis: NCENTER and RCENTER.

Experience, economies of scale, and following the leader effect As elaborated in the conceptual framework, there is a tendency for foreign direct investment to accumulate and cluster in some locations. The underlying mechanism of this process can be attributed to several forces: experience effect, economies of scale, and the follow the leader effect. The quantitative separation of these effects is not practical in this analysis. Rather, only one variable, FDISUM (the accumulated amount of realized foreign direct investment), is used to represent either one of the three effects or the combinations of them.

Recipient city versus void city: differences in policy, location, and position

From coast to periphery: the saturation rates of foreign direct investment recipient cities and the probability of switching from foreign direct investment void to a recipient city

The saturation rate refers to the percentage of foreign direct investment recipient cities in a city group. Five rates can be calculated: saturation rates of port cities, coastal cities, inland cities, and periphery cities and the national average saturation rate. These rates provide a direct way to examine the impact of a city's relative distance from the coast and the home countries, and large urban and industrial centers on its status as a recipient city. Other measures such as the percentages of each type of city within all recipient cities may not be appropriate because the prior probability of different types of cities is not taken into consideration. Table 5.1 shows the difference of the saturation rates between different type of cities.

Three statements can be made based on Table 5.1. First, there was a gradual spatial spread of the presence of foreign direct investment in China until most cities became foreign direct investment recipient cities. In 1985 only a little more than one-half of the cities had foreign direct investment. This rate changed to 98 per cent in 1993. Second, at any given time, the saturation rates decline in order from the coastal port city group, to the coastal city group, to the inland city group, and to the periphery city group. This order also tends to be the order for the saturation rate of

Table 5.1
The saturation rates of foreign direct investment recipient cities within four types of cities, 1984 to 1993[1]

Year	Coastal port cities (16, 15)[2]	Coastal cities (35, 31)	Inland cites (35, 29)	Periphery cities (14, 12)	National average (100, 87)
1984	94	63	37	35	55
1985	94	71	62	50	69
1986	94	80	66	29	70
1987	100	87	58	33	72
1988	100	97	79	41	84
1989	100	100	68	50	83
1990	100	100	83	67	89
1991	100	100	90	67	92
1992	100	100	96	83	96
1993	100	100	96	90	98

1. Due to data constraints, the assessment of the saturation rates are based on two samples. One sample that consists of 100 cities is used for assessing the rates during 1984 to 1986. The rate assessment after 1987 is based on an 87 city sample.
2. The two numbers in parenthesis in each column indicate the number of cities in each category for the 100 and 87 city samples, respectively.

each city group becoming 100 per cent when the presence of foreign direct investment is pervasive in all the cities in a city group.

The implications of these observations are twofold. First, the suitability for being a foreign direct investment recipient city is a relative term. Usually, it would be difficult to declare a city's unsuitability for foreign direct investment, unless the political and social situations make production extremely unstable or impossible. This might be one aspect of the difference between location-decision making at a national level and that at a subnational level. Some factors that make a location an absolutely unsuitable locational choice, e.g., political instability, are assumed away within a subnational context. One may argue that the investment environment of each city changes over time. Cities become suitable because they develop and improve. Yet, the pattern established in Table 5.1 is too strong to attribute the pattern changes to the improvement and development of cities alone. The improvement of the overall investment environment in China might be an even more important factor. Then again, other mechanisms such as the increase and diversification of investors and diminishing investment opportunity can all enter the process. Second, the spatial order of the saturation rate suggests that the distance from the coast is an important factor in foreign investors' decision to exclude cities as alternative locational choices, at least for the time being.

The two implications just stated are substantiated by another statistic of these city groups: the different probabilities of a city becoming a foreign direct investment recipient city within each city group. Table 5.2 shows that at any given point in time, a city in a coastal region was more likely to attract foreign direct investment than a city in periphery regions.

Preferential policy toward foreign direct investment

Applying the same technique, the saturation rate, does not aid us much in understanding foreign investors' preferences for city groups classified by the government's imposed special policy and incentives. The main reason is that by the end of 1983, most of the cities that were later given COC and COR policies in 1984 and 1985 already had a foreign direct investment presence. As such, by the end of 1985 all the cities that had the special policy had the presence of foreign direct investment in varying amounts. Yet, the impact of policy instruments cannot be denied. There are two reasons for this. First, the four special economic zones that did not have much of an advantage over other cities in many other aspects have thrived on foreign direct investment. There would not be Shenzhen and Zhuhai if it were not for the special economic zone policy. Second, the status as a recipient city was not totally stable, especially during abnormal circumstances such as the 1986 crash of foreign direct investment inflow and the 'June 4, 1989 Tiananmen Square Incident.' However, cities that had special policies had been successful in keeping their foreign direct investment recipient status from year to year even during aforementioned abnormal circumstances. Since 1984, the saturation rates of foreign direct investment presence in cities with special policies have been virtually 100 per cent. Unstable cities that switched back from recipient cities to foreign direct investment void cities

79

were usually those with no special policy at all. In 1986, out of nine cities which switched back to foreign direct investment void city status, eight were no-policy cities. Only one was a COC city. In 1989, all the six cities that changed from recipient cities to void cities were no-policy cities.

Up to now, we can conclude that among other factors, distance from the coast with (implications in several aspects) and special government policy and incentives did have some impact on foreign investors' decisions to choose one city group over another as their optional locational choices. Yet, the preferences eroded away when changes in investment environment, structure of foreign investors, and changes in host regions are induced by established foreign direct investment plus their own evolutionary processes.

Statistical discriminant analysis of foreign direct investment void cities and foreign direct investment recipient cities

Having discussed the possible role of policy and location in discriminating foreign direct investment recipient cities from foreign direct investment void cities, we now turn to those urban attributes that can be easily measured on an interval scale. Discriminant analysis[2] is used to analyze the relevancy of each interval variable for the presence of foreign direct investment. Discriminant analysis is a statistical technique that allows one to study two or more groups of objects with respect to a

---

Table 5.2
Relative frequency of turning into a recipient city in each city group

Year	Port City	Coastal City	Inland City	Periphery City	National Average
1985	0.00	0.31	0.50	0.22	0.38
1986	0.00	0.60	0.31	0.00	0.32
1988	N/A*	0.75	0.58	0.13	0.46
1989	N/A	1.00	0.33	0.29	0.36
1990	N/A	N/A	0.56	0.33	0.47
1991	N/A	N/A	0.60	0.25	0.44
1992	N/A	N/A	0.61	0.50	0.57

* After all the cities in a city group become foreign direct investment recipient cities, relative frequency of new recipient cities emerged from is not applicable to this group.

80

host of variables simultaneously. These variables are also called discriminating factors. Discriminant functions are created so maximum group differences can be achieved. A score is then calculated for each object by using the discriminant functions with respect to its values on the relevant discriminating factors. The scores for two objects of different groups are expected to be as different as possible. The standardized canonical coefficients in the discriminating functions tell us the importance of each variable in calculating the discriminant score for each object.

Yet there is a limitation to using the canonical coefficients to explain the importance of each discriminating factor because of the correlations among variables in the discriminant functions. As such, the structural coefficients, which are simply bivariate correlations between discriminant scores and variables, usually provide better guidance about which factor is more important in separating the groups apart. The variables that have higher structural coefficients are the more important discriminating factors.

Table 5.3 lists the discriminating functions for respective years. Table 5.4 lists the total structural coefficients for each discriminant function. By combining the results in both tables, the following observations are warranted.

First, the important factors that differentiate the two city groups are the city size factors (OUTPUT, RETAILVAL, MP), the condition of the infrastructure (AVEPIPE), the level of urbanization (URBANPOP%) and the level of industrialization (OUTPUT%).

Second, the factors that differentiate between the two groups most changes over time. Table 5.4 reveals that there were three phases of change. During 1985 and 1986, it was the size of the local market and the size of urban economic activity that made the difference. This shows that, foreign investors exclude small cities as the possible location choices for their local production. During the years 1987 to 1990, however, the condition of the urban infrastructure became the leading discriminating factor. The size of local markets took second place. This says that new foreign direct investment commitment each year during this period was more likely made to the cities that had better urban infrastructures instead of the size of the local market. The 1991 pattern suggests the start of another phase in which foreign investors' decisions to exclude some cities from their lists of possible locational choices was likely based on the market potential of the cities. In other words, if a city is in a province that has greater provincial retail sales and is geographically closer to other major markets at the provincial level, it would probably become a foreign direct investment recipient city. A better infrastructure was a good discriminator second only to market potential. Considering the spatial pattern of market potential, this means that the populous provinces such as Sichuan Province started to gain foreign investors' attention since 1991.

Table 5.3

Foreign direct investment void city versus foreign direct investment recipient city, the discriminant functions*

1985	1986	1987	1988	1990	1991
VALADD% (-1.50)	RETAILVAL (1.62)	RETAILVAL (1.23)	AVEPIPE (1.14)	FDISUM (-1.84)	AVEWOKOUT (-1.64)
RETAILVAL (1.16)	OUTPUT (-0.95)	AVEPIPE (0.99)	FDISUM86 (-0.84)	AVERETAIL (1.32)	WAGE (1.24)
AVEWOKOUT (0.99)	AVERETAIL (0.74)	FDISUM86 (-0.85)	RETAILVAL (0.70)	VALADD% (-0.96)	VALADD% (1.10)
OUTPUT (-0.86)	GAP (0.59)	RESIDOUT% (0.67)	WAGE (0.43)	RATEOUT (-0.68)	RESIDOUT% (0.58)
TAXWELL (0.63)	FDISUM84 (-0.50)	OUTPUT (-0.61)	RATEPIPE (0.36)	RETAILVAL (0.65)	AVEPIPE (-0.44)
MP (-0.40)		RATERETL (0.44)		AVEPIPE (0.60)	RATEOUT (0.28)
OUTPUT% (0.31)		%OUTPUT (-0.29)		AVEWOKOUT (0.59)	MP84 (-0.27)
		TAXWELL (0.27)		GAP (0.44)	RATEPIPE (-0.24)

*1. One function is built for each year.
2. Each entry in this table consists of the discriminant factor name and its standardized canonical discriminant function coefficient.

Table 5.4

Foreign direct investment void city versus foreign direct investment recipient city: the total structural coefficients*

1985	1986	1987	1988	1990	1991
RETAILVAL (0.59)	RETAILVAL (0.74)	AVEPIPE (0.64)	AVEPIPE (0.65)	AVEPIPE (0.51)	MP84 (-0.51)
OUTPUT (0.47)	OUTPUT (0.51)	RETAILVAL (0.53)	RETAILVAL (0.51)	VALADD% (-0.47)	AVEPIPE (-0.46)
AVERETAIL 0.41	OUTPUT% (0.51)	RESIDOUT% (0.47)	OUTPUT (0.47)	RETAILVAL (0.40)	URBANPOP% (0.45)
OUTPUT% (0.40)	GAP (0.47)	VALADD% (-0.47)	FDISUM86 (0.36)	GAP (0.36)	GAP (-0.39)
FDISUM84 (0.40)	AVEPIPE (0.50)	OUTPUT (0.43)	RATEPIPE (0.35)	OUTPUT (0.34)	VALADD% (0.38)
TAXWELL (0.39)	FDISUM84 (0.36)	MP84 (0.32)	AVERETAIL (0.28)	RATERETL (0.22)	RETAILVAL (-0.32)
AVEPIPE (0.34)	AVERETAIL (0.35)	URBANPOP% (-0.26)	VALADD% (-0.26)	AVERETAIL (0.22)	AVEWOKOUT(-0.29)
VALADD% (-0.33)	URBANPOP% (-0.34)	RATERETL (0.25)	RESIDOUT% (0.21)	URBANPOP% (-0.22)	OUTPUT (-0.28)
RESIDOUT% (0.29)	RESIDOUT% (0.30)	RATEOUT (0.21)	AVEWOKOUT (0.19)	MP84 (0.22)	RATEOUT (-0.25)
WAGE (-0.23)	MP84 (0.31)	GAP (0.15)	WAGE(0.19)	FDISUM88 (0.20)	FDISUM88 (-0.25)
MP84 (-0.21)	VALADD% (-0.23)	RATEPIPE (0.10)	MP84(0.17)	RESIDOUT% (0.18)	OUTPUT% (0.21)
URBANPOP% (0.13)	AVEWOKOUT (0.01)	AVEWOKOUT (0.06)	OUTPUT% (0.10)	RATEOUT (-0.10)	AVERETAIL (-0.19)
AVEWOKOUT (-0.09)	WAGE (-0.10)	WAGE (-0.07)	TAXWELL (-0.07)	AVEWOKOUT (0.14)	RATEPIPE (-0.15)
GAP (-0.07)	TAXWELL (0.02)	OUTPUT% (0.09)	RATERETL (-0.06)	WAGE (0.15)	WAGE (0.03)
		TAXWELL (0.00)	RATEOUT (0.05)	RATEPIPE (-0.11)	RESIDOUT% (-0.09)
			URBANPOP% (-0.04)	OUTPUT% (-0.01)	TAXWELL (-0.08)
			GAP (-0.00)	TAXWELL (0.01)	RATERETL (-0.06)

* This table presents the bivariate relationships between discriminatory variables and discriminant functions. It shows which variable is more relevant to either one of the city groups: foreign direct investment void city and foreign direct investment recipient city.

Conclusion

By combining the analysis on both nominal and interval factors, we can draw some conclusions on the factors that discriminate a city's potential to become a foreign direct investment recipient city. It was discovered that both the special policy toward foreign direct investment and city location affected a city's possibility of becoming a foreign direct investment recipient city. Higher percentages of cities found closer to the coastline were foreign direct investment recipient cities. Cities that were foreign direct investment void in a previous period yet found closer to the coastline were also more likely to become a recipient city in the following period. Cities that retained special policy and preferential treatment for foreign direct investment were more successful in keeping their status than those that did not. All these trends were consistent over time. These suggest that the special policy and ease of interaction with home countries as well as national and large regional urban centers did affect foreign investors' decisions as to choosing one group of cities over another as possible locational choices.

By taking into consideration these results, the following generalizations can be made. First, during 1985 and 1986, being closer to the coast, a special policy, and a larger local market was most relevant for a city to attract any amount of foreign direct investment. This conclusion may also be extended to the time period before 1984. Second, from 1987 until 1990, cities farther from the coast and/or with an underdeveloped urban infrastructure were unlikely to attract foreign investors' commitments. Third, within 1991, both a city's market potential and its location from the coast made a difference in its status about whether or not it would be a foreign direct investment recipient city. It is unnecessary to extend the trend revealed in 1991 to the period after 1991, as virtually every city (at the prefecture level or above) had varying amounts of foreign direct investment committed each year.

Notes

1   The equation for calculating market potential is as follow: $MP_i = \sum(P_j/D_{ij})$. MP_i is the market potential for a city in the province i. Pj is the retail value of province j. D_{ij} is the distance between province i and province j. Both i and j are from 1 to 30. There are three assumptions underlying this calculation. First, it is not in the belief of these authors that a city can practically form a separate market, no matter from a geographical, demographical, or a socioeconomic point view. Separate markets at the provincial level, on the other hand, do exist due to traditional and behavioral bases for market segmentation. Second, although various trade barriers (theoretical nonexistence) exist among provinces, these barriers do not enter foreign investors' decisions. The only thing that deters a venture from selling its product from one province to another is the distance friction effect.

2   See *Discriminant Analysis*, by William R. Klecka, Sage Publications: Beverly Hills, 1980.

6 Location of FDI at the prefecture city level: a statistical analysis

Introduction

In the last chapter, the presence of foreign direct investment was examined. The focus was on finding the urban characteristics that makes a city become a recipient of foreign direct investment. This chapter, however, examines the urban attributes that determine the spatial distribution of foreign direct investment. In other words, the focus is what makes a city attract more foreign direct investment. Of course, this analysis is based on the framework laid out in Chapter Three. The statistical technique is multiple regression analysis.

One should note the underlying assumption of this chapter's analysis: that there is homogeneity of foreign direct investment in respective periods of time. In other words, the impact of locational determinants on every dollar of foreign direct investment is assumed to be the same. In this way, we can talk about what determines the location of foreign direct investment overall. This assumption can also be described within the locational framework. That is why we ignore the multidimensional quality of the first dimension, FSVs, and focus on the second, LSVs, and the third, the temporal and dynamic dimension.

The analysis in this chapter is as follows. One, a cross temporal analysis is conducted for each year after 1985 by using both the factual variable model and the latent variable model. Then these cross-section analyzes are compared to uncover the dynamic changes of the location models over time. Additional attention is paid to elaborating on the implications of the dummy variables in the models. After that, the conclusions on the major locational determinants of foreign direct investment in China and the dynamic changes over time are drawn.

Model specification: exponential model and product model

Based on preliminary analysis, different model specifications are applied to latent and factual variable regression analyses. The criteria for this model selection are simplicity of explanation and effectiveness of modeling for variance explained by independent variables. A product model (equation 6.1) is used for regression analysis on urban latent variables:

$$Y=a(\prod_1^n X^{b_i})$$ (6.1)

with Y as the amount of foreign direct investment pledged each year in US dollars, X_i as i^{th} urban latent variable, and both a and b_i as coefficients. This equation can be transformed into the following linear equation required in multiple regression analysis by taking the logarithm of each side:

$$\log Y = \log a + \sum_1^n (b_i \log X_i)$$ (6.2)

The model used for regression of foreign direct investment on factual urban variables is an exponential model taking the following form:

$$Y = \exp(a + \sum_1^n b_i X_i)$$ (6.3)

Representation of each term is the same as in equation 6.1. Taking the logarithm on both sides, we get a linear equation of the factual variable model used in multiple regression analysis:

$$\log Y = a + \sum_1^n b_i X_i$$ (6.4)

The above model specification and transformation of the original models into linear functions should remind us how to interpret the resulting regression coefficients. All the regression analyzes are designed to find the relationships between a dependant variable (foreign direct investment in US dollars) and the independent variables (either urban latent variables or factual locational variables). After the transformation, however, the direct linear relationships are built between the logarithm of the actual amount of foreign direct investment, rather than the actual amount of foreign direct investment itself, and a host of independent variables.

Latent urban variables

Tables 6.1 to 6.3 show the latent urban variables extracted by factor analysis on the factual urban variables. There is one table for each year of 1984, 1986, and 1991. Each table also shows the major components in each latent variable (factor) and other related statistics. The major components listed under each latent variable are the variables that at least one-half of their variance can be explained by the respective latent variable. The number of factors in each year is selected in light of both the scree-plot and ease of interpretation.

Table 6.1
Latent urban variables for 1984[1]

	CITY SIZE	LEVEL OF URBANIZATION	LEVEL OF DEVELOPMENT	LEVEL OF PRODUCTIVITY
Major Components and coefficients in rotated factor matrix[2]	EMPLOYEE (0.96) RETAILVAL (0.96) ELECTRIC (0.93) OUTPUT (0.93) NETFIXK (0.93) URBANPOP (0.91)	URBANPOP% (0.88) NONAPOP% (0.82) OUTPUT% (0.80) URBANOUT% (0.81) AVELECTRI (0.74) GAP (-0.73)	AVERETAIL (0.95) NETFIXK% (0.90) AVESAVE (0.87) RESIDOUT% (0.86) AVEPIPE (0.78) POLICY (0.77)	AVEWOKOUT (0.93) AVENETOUT (0.93) VALADD% (0.87) AVEFIRMOUT (0.74) KLRATIO (0.68)
Eigenvalue	15.94	7.72	7.23	4.47
Per cent of variance[3]	29.5	14.3	13.4	8.3

1. Total number of variables included in the factor analysis is 54, which covers a wide range of urban characteristics. The number of factors is chosen by the scree plot.
2. Refer to Chapter Five for the explanation for each variable abbreviation. The following is a list of variable abbreviations that are not included in Chapter Five. EMPLOYEE: the total number of employees in state and collectively owned enterprises and institutions. ELECTRIC: total amount of electricity used each year by both industrial sectors and residents. AVELECTRI: electricity consumption per capita per year. NONAPOP%: percentage of population registered as non-agricultural residents. NETFIXK: total net fixed capital. NETFIXK%: percentage of net fixed capital within total fixed capital. SOEOUT%: gross output value of manufacturing industry by state owned enterprise (SOE). AVESAVE: saving per capita in urban area. AVENETOUT: net manufacturing output (value added) per capita. AVEWOKOUT: gross manufacturing output value per worker. NUMPHONE: number of telephone in urban area. AVEPHONE: number of phones per capita in urban area. SCIENCPOP: number of employee having middle or higher level of professional certificates. VALUEADD: value added (net output value) of manufacturing industry. AVEFIRMOUT: gross manufacturing output per firm (state owned and collectively owned: SOEs and COEs). AMOUTPUT: gross output value of agriculture and manufacturing industry. AVEAMOUT: per capita gross output value of agriculture and manufacturing industry. AVEFIRMOUT: per capita gross output value of agriculture and manufacturing industry.
3. The percentage of total variance accounted by the four factors is 65.5 per cent.

89

Table 6.2
Latent urban variable for 1986[1]

	CITY SIZE	LEVEL OF URBANIZATION	LEVEL OF DEVELOPMENT	LEVEL OF PRODUCTIVITY
Major components and coefficient in rotated factor matrix[2]	VALUEADD (0.96) OUTPUT (0.96) RETAILVAL (0.95) NETFIXK (0.95) URBANPOP (0.90)	URBANOUT% (0.85) URBANPOP% (0.82) NONAPOP%(0.78) SOEOUT%(0.77)	AVERETAIL (0.90) AVESAVE (0.89) NETFIXK%(0.89) AVEPIPE (0.79)	AVEWOKOUT (0.92) WAGE (0.79) KLRATIO (0.78) TERTPOP% (0.64)
Eigenvalue	15.29	8.37	7.06	3.60
Per cent of variance[3]	25.1	13.7	11.6	5.9

1. n=61.
2. Refer to Chapter Five for variable abbreviation explanation.
3. Total percentage of variance explained is 56.3 per cent.

Table 6.3
Latent urban variables of 1991[1]

Major components and coefficient in rotated factor matrix[2]	CITY SIZE	LEVEL OF DEVELOPMENT	LEVEL OF URBANIZATION
	RETAILVAL (0.96)	AVEPHONE(0.88)	URBANOUT% (0.81)
	EMPLOYEE (0.96)	AVEOUTPUT (0.87)	URBANPOP% (0.79)
	URBANPOP (0.94)	AVERETAIL (0.87)	NONAPOP%(0.77)
	SCIENCPOP (0.94)	AVEAMOUT (0.86)	RESIDOUT% (-0.71)
	AMOUTPUT(0.93)	WAGE (0.82)	
	OUTPUT (0.92)	RATEOUT (0.75)	
	NUMPHONE (0.92)	POLICY(0.68)	
Eigenvalue	13.37	7.96	6.16
Per cent of variance[3]	25.7	15.3	11.8

1. n=52.
2. Refer to both Chapter 5 and Table 6.2 note 2 for variable abbreviation explanation.
3. Total percentage of variance explained is 52.8 per cent

The number of factors (latent variables) in 1984 (Table 6.1), 1986 (Table 6.2), and 1991(Table 6.3) are four, four, and three, respectively. As revealed from these tables, there were three persistent basic dimensions in China's urban landscape: CITY SIZE, LEVEL OF DEVELOPMENT, and LEVEL OF URBANIZATION[1]. There was also a fourth dimension in the 1984 and 1986 factor analyzes, LEVEL OF PRODUCTIVITY that pertains to the overall labor productivity and wage levels of cities.

CITY SIZE represents one underlying urban dimension shared by such urban factual variables as the number of employees (EMPLOYEE), the total local retail value (RETAILVAL), and the total gross output value of manufacturing industry (OUTPUT). Of course, the most commonly used measure, urban population size (URBANPOP), is also included. Obviously this urban factor (latent variable), CITY SIZE, refers to not only to the physical size of a city, but also to the size of a city in its economy, consumption, and established economic activities. In a case where CITY SIZE was a statistically significant independent variable in explaining the location pattern of foreign direct investment, it implies that foreign direct investment is responsive to any of these aspects or the combination of several or all.

The second underlying dimension of China's urban system is the LEVEL OF URBANIZATION that entails two basic aspects. One is the structural aspect measured by the percentages of urban population (people that live in the urban district) and nonagricultural population (secondary and tertiary employment) within the total city population. Those two percentages can be taken as surrogates for the cities' macroeconomic structure for the division between primary and secondary industries. Another aspect is the physical side of urbanization that concerns the degree of concentration of both people and economic activity in the urban area.

The LEVEL OF DEVELOPMENT, the third underlying dimension in China's urban system, brings our attention to some important urban characteristics expressed as per capita. These characteristics include consumption, income, and urban infrastructure. Higher levels of development reflect both a higher level of purchasing power and higher level of consumption. A combination of CITY SIZE and LEVEL OF DEVELOPMENT provide a good measure for the size of a market.

In the analyzes of 1984 and 1986, a fourth factor is found: LEVEL OF PRODUC-TIVITY. It reflects labor productivity, labor cost, and the capital labor ratio. This dimension further differentiates cities from each other.

Location of foreign direct investment: explanation by latent variable models

Table 6.4 summaries the results of statistical modeling by using urban latent variables. Details of the statistical models are listed in Appendix A. The interpretation of the models follows two basic steps. First, the locational determinants (statistically significant independent variables), their importance, and relationships among them are examined. Second, changes of models over time are registered.

As there are only at most four latent variables, the structure of the latent variable models is obvious. The models spanning from 1985 to 1993 are consistent in that

Table 6.4
Summary of regression analyses of the log of FDI pledged on urban latent variables*

Latent variables	1985	1987	1988	1989	1990	1991	1993
LEVEL OF DEVELOPMENT	+0.59, 0.31	+0.59, 0.33	+0.49, 0.21	+0.56, 0.30	+0.61, 0.35	+0.60, 0.35	+0.45, 0.22
CITY SIZE	+0.40, 0.16	+0.39, 0.15	+0.47, 0.20	+0.48, 0.21	+0.48, 0.22	+0.47, 0.22	+0.86, 0.34
LEVEL OF PRODUCTIVITY			+0.39, 0.16	+0.23, 0.06	+0.27, 0.07	+0.19, 0.06	
LEVEL OF URBANIZATION				-0.18, 0.03	-0.23, 0.05	-0.25, 0.04	-0.20, 0.04
r squared	0.47	0.48	0.57	0.60	0.69	0.67	0.60

* 1. 1985 model is based on 1984 urban latent variables. As for models during 1987 to 1991 and 1993, models are based on 1986 and 1991 urban latent variables, respectively.
2. The first signed number in a cell is the coefficient for standardized data. The second number is the increase of r squared when a variable enters the equation. The sequence from larger to smaller also indicates the sequence of variables entering the equation.
3. The last row is the total r squared for each model.
4. Empty cells mean that the respective latent variable is not in the model for that year.

DEVELOPMENT and CITY SIZE are the main explanatory variables. Both are positively associated with the amount of pledged foreign direct investment. In other words, the foreign direct investment each year can be explained by these two latent variables.

Between these two variables, the LEVEL OF DEVELOPMENT is more pertinent to the independent variable for most of the models (1985 to 1991). In the 1993 model, CITY SIZE appears as the most important explanatory variable. No matter which latent variable enters the model first, the first and most important variable alone always explains more than 30 per cent of the spatial variation in the dependent variable.

By comparing the model formulation changes through the years, one can detect two tendencies. One is the increase of the effectiveness of the models, i.e. the coefficient of determination (r^2) increases from 0.47 in 1984 to 0.67 in 1991. Another is the number of variables included in the formulations increases over time. Between 1985 and 1987, out of the four latent variables, only two are included in the model formulations. By 1988, all available latent variables are relevant for inducing foreign direct investment. Although it is not totally conclusive, the implications of these two trends are not to be overlooked. In the first place, this suggests that the experience effect became active. Over time, as foreign investors acquired more knowledge about China's investment environment, investment decisions became more rational. More factors were taken into consideration in their investment decision making. By further looking into the composition of each year's new investment commitment, the experience could be further exemplified in two forms. Each year's new commitment consists of two parts: new investment committed by first-time investors in China, and sequential commitment made by those who already had establishments in China. In each case, there was no denial of the experience effect. For those who had operating experience in China, their increased knowledge was acquired first hand. For those who had been interested in business expansion into China and only started to commit themselves, the longer period of observation on China's investment environment and the performance of other already committed investors made them more knowledgeable in their decision making process.

The second explanation may be the diversification of foreign investors and changing characteristics of foreign direct investment in size and industrial composition. The changes in these aspects would induce the change of locational requirements for foreign direct investment as a whole.

The third explanation is that the changes are statistical proof of the spatial diffusion of foreign direct investment in China. Over the years, the total volume of foreign direct investment inflow increased, so did the extent of its spatial distribution. At early stages, limited amounts of foreign direct investment concentrated in a small number of cities that were relatively homogeneous. Later as more investment poured in, the threshold for a suitable location lowered and foreign direct investment expanded into a broader geographical space. As the recipient locations became more diversified and could be distinguished from each other in more dimensions, the locational model became more complex.

It would be ideal if the impact of these sources on the changes of model formulation and effectiveness could be separated. Data problems prevent further analysis on the first and the third sources of influence. Without a detailed firm list of pledged foreign direct investment each year, the pledged foreign direct investment for each year cannot be further classified into totally new investment and sequential investment. For the third source, the part of pledged foreign direct investment that is going to be located in new cities can be isolated. Yet, this kind of data partition renders less than enough cases for model building to reveal the difference of location patterns between new foreign direct investment recipient cities and established foreign direct investment recipient cities. The impact from the second source, foreign direct investment country of origin, is discussed in the next chapter. Though the impact of these sources on the model changes cannot be separated practically, the very existence of these effects cannot be denied.

Location of foreign direct investment: the factual variable models

Having discussed the models using latent variables, we turn to statistical locational models built upon factual location-specific variables. Table 6.5 summarises the models detailed in Appendix B. Before we further discuss the implications of these models, we first look at what the models tell us.

By looking at Table 6.5, one can see that no two models are the same. Yet, by comparing the models over the years, several trends emerge. First, for most of the models, the most important explanatory variable is a size variable (mostly RETAILVAL but URBANPOP for 1987 and 1988) and one policy variable. Except for 1987 and 1989, the size variable usually enters the model formulations first and explains at least one quarter or as much as 34 per cent of total variance in the logarithm of pledged foreign direct investment each year.

Second, the importance of dummy variables in these models is apparent. In most of the models (before 1991), the second most important variable is the SEZPOLICY that explains at least around 15 to 20 per cent of the variance in the dependent variable. This signals the importance of SEZs as recipient locations for foreign direct investment. Other statistically important dummy variables are other policy variables and location and distance indicator variables. The persistence of the impact of a city as a regional economic and urban center through the years is also clear. The ways that a regional or national economic center affects the inflow of foreign direct investment is not that all clear. It may be the infrastructure, the economies of scale, or the existing industrial and economic establishment. In fact, this inconclusiveness of the dummy variables is typical of most of the dummy variables. This will be dealt with later in the analysis of these factual variable models. The predominance of dummy variables in these models, at least in number, altered starting in 1992 when the growth rate of total retail value during 1986 to 1991 took over the place of the SEZ policy variable in most of the previous models.

Third, while policy and urban center dummy variables are relevant through the years, the impact of social and physical distances from home countries is relevant

Table 6.5
Summary of regression analyses of FDI pledged on factual locational variables*

Variables	1985	1986	1987	1988	1989	1990	1991	1992	1992-1993
RETAILVAL	+0.40 (0.26)	+0.53 (0.34)			+0.37 (0.13)	+0.38 (0.28)	+0.36 (0.27)	+0.29 (0.28)	+0.31 (0.33)
URBANPOP			+0.32 (0.11)	+0.44 (0.23)					
SEZPOLICY	+0.27 (0.17)	+0.23 (0.11)		+0.35 (0.21)	+0.38 (0.08)	+0.51 (0.22)	+0.51 (0.21)		
COCPOLICY	+0.19 (0.03)			+0.26 (0.08)		+0.33 (0.08)	+0.37 (0.08)		+0.28 (0.04)
CORPOLICY						+0.22 (0.06)	+0.24 (0.09)		+0.21 (0.04)
DSADJACEN	+0.35 (0.06)	+0.24 (0.05)		+0.21 (0.03)					
DCPORT					+0.36 (0.29)			+0.27 (0.05)	
DCCOAST		-0.27 (0.05)							
DCINLAND	-0.19 (0.06)		-0.24 (0.06)						

Table 6.5
Summary of regression analyses of foreign direct investment pledged on factual locational variables*
(continued)

Variables	1985	1986	1987	1988	1989	1990	1991	1992	1992-1993
RCENTER	+0.22 (0.03)	+0.24 (0.04)		+0.28 (0.05)	+0.21 (0.05)	+0.18 (0.02)	+0.19 (0.03)	+0.27 (0.07)	+0.20 (0.07)
MP	-0.38 (0.05)					-0.17 (0.02)			
FDISUM			+0.43 (0.28)						
KLRATIO				+0.17 (0.03)					
VALADD%						-0.14 (0.02)			
RATERETL								+0.29 (0.15)	+0.32 (0.12)
TAXWELL								+0.16 (0.03)	+0.15 (0.02)
R squared	0.65	0.59	0.45	0.63	0.59	0.70	0.68	0.58	0.63

* 1. Each cell contains two statistics on each variable within different year's model. The first number is the standardized coefficient. The number in parenthesis is the unique contribution to the r squared when the variable enters a model. The variable with the largest number in parenthesis enters a model first.

mainly before 1989. In other words, adjacency to Hong Kong and having strong social ties with Hong Kong and overseas Chinese investors as a whole had been partially responsible for explaining the overall location pattern of foreign direct investment in China. This may attest to the evidence presented in the overview chapter that Guangdong Province and a few others predominantly accommodated most of the foreign direct investment commitments before 1990. The location variables (DCPORT, DCCOAST, DCINLAND, and DCREMOTE) that are to reflect the effect of distance from home countries were also statistically relevant, but rather sporadic. The negative impact of inland location contrary to the positive impact of coastal port location is fully expected, as coastal port cities stand at advantageous points in interaction, for both material and information flows, with home countries.

The above observations concern the overall patterns of the models. We know the importance of a city size variable in all the models. The importance of dummy variables (concerning a city's location, distance from home country, and position in the urban system) in most models is also acknowledged. It is time to turn our attention to the most interesting aspect of these models, the structure of the policy variables in a model and its change over time. This aspect was already mentioned in the above second observation when SEZ policy is seen as the second most important explanatory factor in most models. But there is more in the impact of policy expressed by these factual variable models.

The structure of the policy variables refers to the composition of the three types of special policies and preferential treatments toward foreign direct investment: SEZ policy, COC policy, and COR policy. Their basic components and the sequence of their application and their spatial coverage were discussed in Chapter Four. The order from SEZ policy to COR policy is also the order of use and the order of the levels of preferential treatment toward foreign direct investment. The reverse of this order is the size of the spatial coverage of each policy, from smallest to largest. The following can be said about the structure and structural changes of these policy variables:

1   For most of the models, at least one policy variable is present as the second variable entering the models and contributes significantly to the explanation of the dependent variable. This is a clear indication of the persistent impact of government policy on the location decision of foreign investors.

2   Out of the three types of open door policy, SEZ policy (initiated in late 1978) is the most influential. This is shown by its persistent presence in most models and most of the time being the second most important explanatory variable.

3   The coastal open city policy (COCPOLICY) was quick to surface in the 1985 model considering that it was only initiated in 1984. One should be reminded that 1985 was the year of a short-lived boom of foreign direct investment commitment in the middle 1980s. While SEZPOLICY kept showing up even during the crash of foreign direct investment commitment

in 1986, the impact of COCPOLICY was absent for 1986 and 1987 and reemerged in 1989.[2] This is the statistical evidence of the temporary retreat of foreign investors to their familiar territory, SEZs, after the tentative venturing to COC cities during the boom. However, the impressive legal and policy advance and improvement of investment environment after the crash of foreign direct investment commitment in China overall and in COC cities in specific, made the COC policy relevant again in 1989.

4   1990 is a dividing year when all three types of open door policies established their statistical relevancy in foreign investors' locational decision making process. In the first four years after its initiation, the COR policy did not have much appeal to foreign investors, at least statistically. Considering the crash of the boom in 1986, the tentative recovery during 1987 to 1988, and the 1989 'Tiananmen Square Incident', the lag of the impact of COR policy is totally justified. The statistical relevancy of the full spectrum of open door policy lasted for two years. It signaled the start of a full fledged foreign direct investment inflow and the spatial dispersion of foreign direct investment in coastal regions.

5   Only a two-year span from 1990 separates another important change in the models. This time it is the absence of SEZ policy in the model. With the two most important variables being the size of the local market and its growth rate in the past years before 1991, the absence of the SEZPOLICY variable strongly suggests the over concentration of foreign direct investment in SEZs was no longer statistically significant in the overall spatial pattern of foreign direct investment commitment in China. It is not a surprise, though, to see the continuing presence of COC policy and COR policy in the locational models in 1992 to 1993. These two types of policy still cover most of China's coastal area, their relevancy in the overall spatial location pattern of foreign direct investment is expected to continue in years to come.

6   If not more, the replacement of SEZPOLICY variable by the rate of market growth as the second most important explanatory variable in 1992 to 1993 provides just as much evidence as the absence of SEZPOLICY as to the model changes since 1992. With the size of the local market as the first factor into the model, this variable of market growth rate only proves the location pattern of foreign direct investment commitment started to enter a mature stage where the location of foreign direct investment is affected by the inherited or built-up merits rather than the more volatile aspect of a city: government policy.

After the above discussion of the major trends and elaboration of the policy structures of the factual variable models, a brief conclusion concerning the locational model of foreign direct investment as a whole is warranted. In brief, factual variable location models reveal that other than the size of a city measured in retail value, the

99

open door policy blessed by the central government had been the most important factor in the locational decision of foreign investors in the first ten years. Although the structure of the policy components in each year's model differs, the predominance of SEZ policy persisted. This situation only started to change since 1992 when the rate of market growth replaced the SEZ policy as the second important explanatory variable. Other factors such as a city's position in China's national and regional urban systems and distances from the coast and home countries also affect its attractiveness of as a foreign direct investment recipient location at different periods.

Cutting through the surface: the implication of dummy variables and reinterpretation of the factual variable models

Previous sections revealed the location patterns based on two different approaches. Latent variable models assume that the spatial distribution of foreign direct investment commitment is affected by several fundamental characteristics of China's urban system. Foreign investors may not respond to some specific locational attributes directly. Instead, their locational decisions were based on their comprehension of a city's fundamental attributes. Thus, locational models using urban latent variables enable us to transcend the instability and complexity that factual variable models may have and to grasp the more abstract or the underlying dimensions of the locational mechanism of foreign direct investment. Factual variable models, on the other hand, assume the direct responses of foreign investors to some specific locational attributes.

Three questions follow, though, about any of the locational models. First, are the variables in the models a true indiction of locational determinants of foreign direct investment? Second, do the two approaches tell different stories as far as locational determinants of foreign direct investment are concerned. And third, why don't other theoretically selected variables surface in factual variable models? Only after these questions have been answered, can the true dimensions and locational determinants of foreign direct investment be explained.

For the latent variable models, the independent variables are calculated indices of a number of correlated factual variables. By referring to the first three tables in this chapter, one can reflect on what a latent variable entails when it is included in a model. For factual variable models, however, this is more problematic because of the dummy variables. Their statistical significance may represent the effect of more factors than they are supposed to convey. The dummy variables are just labels of a city's location, foreign direct investment special policy status, or distance from home countries. As these aspects are not suitable to quantitative measurement on interval scales, they are represented by dummy variables. If the grouping of cities by these dummy variables, e.g., by policy dummy variables, happen to be distinctive from each other in more ways than those suggested by the dummy variables, we cannot conclude definitely whether the presence of a dummy variable shows the impact that it is supposed to portray. Or it may just be a representation of the impact of other factual differences between these city groups. In brief, factual models may not be what they appear to be. To counter this problem, the rest of this section is solely

100

Table 6.6

Summary of the implications of policy variables expressed by the spatial variation of other locational variables**

Locational Variables	1984 (0,3) ANOVA test	1984 (0,2) ANOVA test	1986 (0,3) ANOVA test	1986 (0,2) ANOVA test	1991 (0,3) ANOVA test	1991 (0,2) ANOVA test
URBANPOP			*	*	*	*
RETAILVAL	*	*	*	*	*	*
OUTPUT	*	*	*	*	*	*
MP	*	*	*	*	*	*
FDISUM	*		*	*	*	*
AVERETAIL	*		*		*	
AVEWOKOUT			*		*	
WAGE	*		*	*	*	*
AVEPIPE			*	*	*	*
URBANPOP%			*	*	*	*
VALADD%			*	*	*	
RESIDOUT%	*	*	*	*	*	*
RATEOUT			*	*	*	
RATERETL			*		*	

** 1. This is a summary table of the ANOVA tests detailed in Appendix C.

2. ANOVA (0,3) test refers to the ANOVA tests that include all cities of four different types, e.g. cities with no preferential policy toward foreign direct investment, cities with COR policy, cities with COC policy, and cities with SEZ policy. ANOVA (0,2) tests refer to tests that do not include SEZ policy cities. The reason for this division is that there are only four SEZ cities. The exclusion of SEZ cities in ANOVA (0,2) analysis enable us to make a rough assessment as to the impact of SEZ cities on ANOVA (0,3) analysis and extend the implication of policy variables with greater confidence.

3. The single star sign as an entry in a cell indicates that there is a significant difference (at five per cent error level) among different types of cities in measurements labeled in the first column. As mentioned in the title of this table, these measurements are also the ones used as independent variables in the locational modeling.

devoted to determining the implication of dummy variables in factual variable models and reinterpretation of several typical models.

The three policy dummy variables are the focus of the following discussion because of their importance in the factual variable models. Table 6.6 presents a summary of these aspects that are distinct among city groups of different policy status. The distinct differences among four groups of cities (cities with SEZ policy, COC policy, COR policy, and no-special policy) are expressed by their difference in the same interval variable set. Changes over time (1984, 1986, and 1991) can be discerned by reading across rows. The following are some major points suggested by Table 6.6.

First, there are distinct differences between these city groups in their size as measured in either urban population (URBANPOP), gross output value of manufacturing industry (OUTPUT), or total retail value (RETAILVAL). Significant distinctions also exist in their market potential (MP) and level of urbanization (URBANPOP%). Climbing up the policy scale in their favorable treatment and liberal attitude toward foreign direct investment, i.e., no special policy, COR policy, and COC policy, city averages on these aspects increase. This is not surprising since these differences were also part of the rationale when the Chinese government designed the spatial framework of preferential policy toward foreign direct investment. It was argued that coastal cities, especially the fourteen COCs, have better economic and technological infrastructure and have easier access to both domestic and international markets. Therefore, they are poised to be more suitable to absorb the advanced technology brought by foreign direct investment and take part in the international production process. Special policy toward foreign direct investment, then, was granted to these coastal cities to channel foreign direct investment to these cities.

Second, there were distinctly different levels of consumption (AVERETAIL) between SEZs and the rest. There is no statistical evidence to show that consumption levels were different among COCs, CORs and the rest of the cities.

Third, the total amount of realized foreign direct investment also differentiates between cities with different foreign direct investment policies. Up to 1984, SEZs had a disproportional amount of realized foreign direct investment that made them distinguishable from other cities. By 1986, however, the differences in the amount of accumulated foreign direct investment also became significant among cities with COC and COR policies and cities with no special policy.

Fourth, the difference in labor cost among cities was not significant until 1986 and that only existed between SEZs and other cities. The wage gap among cities increased after 1986 and was evidenced by the significant difference that existed in 1991 urban statistics. By then, the wage gap not only existed between SEZs and other cities, but was also present among other city types under foreign direct investment policy, with SEZs having the highest wage level. Contrary to other aspects, this higher labor cost should work to the disadvantages of MNEs, if it is not going to be compensated in other ways, e.g., by higher level of labor productivity.

Fifth, in the same way as accumulated foreign direct investment, the difference in urban infrastructure measured in length of underground pipes per capita (AVEPIPE)

102

was also significant since 1986, with SEZs and COCs having the most advanced infrastructures.

Considering all these aspects, it can be generalized that SEZs, COC cities, and COR cities command more advantages in most of these aspects over cities with no preferential policy. In other words, it works to the advantage of MNEs to place their production in regions with special policies. It is reasonable to assume that foreign investors might have been encouraged to invest in cities with special policies for more than just the preferential treatments they can enjoy. The advanced and large scale of

---

Table 6.7
Implications of being either a national or a regional urban center

Locational variables	Mean compared[2]	1984	1986	1991
URBANPOP	>	*	*	*
RETAILVAL	>	*	*	*
OUTPUT	>	*	*	*
MP	>		*	*
FDISUM	>			*
GAP	<			*
AVERETAIL	>			*
WAGE	>			*
AVEPIPE	>		*	
TAXWELL	>	*		
OUTPUT%	>	*	*	*
RATERETL	>		*	

1. This table is a one way analysis of variance between two group of cities: regional and national centers (gross industrial output greater than 80, 90, 200 million RMB in 1984, 1986, and 1991, respectively).
2. The means for regional and national centers are compared with those of cities other than a national or regional urban centre.
3. A star in a cell indicates various means are significantly different between the two groups of cities at a five per cent error level.

---

established economies, large amounts of accumulated foreign direct investment, and easy access to China's domestic market might also be part of the reason that foreign direct investment had been proportionally concentrated in cities with special policies.

Besides policy variables, Table 6.7 shows that NCENTER or RCENTER (being either a national or a regional urban center) also has important implications. It is shown that for most years in the 1980s, being a national and regional urban center meant having a higher level of industrialization and larger market potential. It also meant size advantages measured in urban population, retail value, and gross industrial output. For 1991 and afterwards, being a national center also meant a larger amount of accumulated foreign direct investment, a higher level of consumption, a higher labor cost, and a smaller gap of development between its urban and peripherial areas.

Table 6.8 shows the distinctions that existed among four city groups classified by the distance from the coast. Besides their larger sizes measured in various terms, cities closer to the sea also possessed better infrastructures (AVEPIPE) and a diversified economy (RESIDOUT%) in terms of ownership structure. Added to this list of advantages since 1986 was the level of accumulated foreign direct investment

Table 6.8
Implications of distance from coast

Locational variable	1984	1986	1991
RETAILVAL	*	*	*
OUTPUT	*	*	*
MP	*	*	*
FDISUM		*	*
AVERETAIL		*	*
WAGE			*
AVEPIPE	*	*	*
VALADD%		*	
RESIDOUT%	*	*	*
RATERETL			*

* Cities are classified into four categories: coastal port city, coastal city, inland city, and city in remote provinces.

(FDISUM), a higher level of consumption (AVERETAIL), and a higher growth rate of their consumer markets (RATERETL). Of course, higher consumption level and its growth rate were accompanied by a higher wage level.

Slightly different from the implication of the above three grouping schemes, some trends of convergence are detected between cities in Guangdong and Fujian Provinces on the one hand, and the rest of cities on the other hand in the late 1980s (Table 6.9). The advantage of being close to home countries (smaller social and physical distances) always includes a higher level of consumption and higher level of accumulated foreign direct investment since 1984. Other advantages of cities in Guangdong and Fujian Provinces commanded in 1984, such as more developed infrastructure and a higher proportion of private economy started to disappear after 1986. Nevertheless, they distinguished themselves from the rest of country again in the rate of economic growth and consumption in 1991.

Having discussed what it really means if a dummy variable appears in a model, it is now possible to give the factual variable models a second look. Several models are picked for detailed analysis as they represent the locational trend under normal circumstances. These years include 1985, 1990, and 1992 to 1993. While trying to pinpoint as closely as possible the real contents of a dummy variable, the following basic assumption is made. The impact of a certain aspect of cities should be captured exclusively by the corresponding interval variable that enters the model first. This

---

Table 6.9
Implications of distance from home country variables*

Locational variables	1984	1986	1991
FDISUM	*	*	*
AVERETAIL	*	*	*
AVEWOKOUT		*	
WAGE		*	*
AVEPIPE	*	*	
RESIDOUT%	*	*	
RATEOUT			*
RATERETL			*

* The effect of distance (social and physical) from a home country is tested between cities in Guangdong and Fujian Province as a group and the rest as another.

Table 6.10
Possible determinants in the locational model for 1985[1]

Locational Variables	RETAIL-VAL	SEZ-POLICY	DS-ADJACEN	MP (-)	DC-INLAND (-)	RCENTER	COC-POLICY
URBANPOP						*	
RETAILVAL	XX	0			*	*	*
OUTPUT		*			*	*	*
MP84		X		XX	*		*
FDISUM		X	X				
AVERETAIL		X	X				
AVEPIPE		X	X		X		
RESIDOUT%		X	X		X		X
OUTPUT%						X	
TAXWELL						X	

1. The first row are the independent variables in 1985 locational model. They are arranged from left to right according to their sequence of entry to the model. The first column are those factual variables that demonstrate significant spatial differences among groups of cities classified according to all the dummy variables in the model.
2. XX indicates a interval independent variable in the model.
3. * indicates there is significant difference among city groups classified by the dummy variable. The difference is measured by the corresponding variable in the leftmost column. However, the impact of this difference on the dependent variable of the locational model is encountered by interval independent variables in the model.
4. X indicates the possible effects carried by the dummy variables in addition to what they are supposed to convey.
5. The sign of a variable's coefficient in a model.

106

assumption is made possible by considering the property of a stepwise multiple regression model. Variables in each model relate to the dependent variable at different levels. The one that takes the first place in the model has the highest correlation with the dependent variable and makes the largest unique contribution to the variance of the dependent variable. The increase of r^2 (the coefficient of determination) made by the second variable after the first one is its unique contribution. Its explanatory power may be larger than what is reflected by its unique contribution to the r^2, because part of its correlation with the dependent variable may be already countered by the first variable if they happen to correlate to each other.

If the second variable happens to be a dummy variable with many implications, we can exclude certain aspects by applying the logic revealed in the last paragraph. This can be illustrated by the following hypothetical example. Suppose both URBANPOP (interval variable) and DCPORT (dummy variable) are the first and second variable in a model. Further suppose that DCPORT also reflects the distinct difference between port cities and the rest of cities as to the size of population (URBANPOP) and level of consumption (AVERETAIL). DCPORT as a dummy variable is the same as if it were labeled the difference between coastal port cities and the rest of the cities. It is purposely designed to reflect the impact of the ease of interaction with home countries on foreign investors' locational decisions. Now with the distinct difference in the urban population size and consumption level between the two groups of cities represented by DCPORT, we hesitate to conclude that the inclusion of DCPORT reveals exactly what it is supposed to be. The impact of different population size and level of consumption is strongly implied. However, with the first variable in the equation being URBANPOP, we can exclude the implication of population size differences between the groups of cities in DCPORT, as it should be countered by URBANPOP. Only in this fashion, can we state that the r^2 increase brought by DCPORT represents the effect of the ease of interaction with home countries, and possibly the consumption level of the local market. This logic can be extended to a dummy in the third place and so forth.

By adopting the above logic, a matrix (table) is created for each of three models (Tables 6.10 to 6.12). Across the first row of each table, listed are the variables in the locational model of the respective year by order of importance and sequence of entering the model. Listed in the first column of each table are those urban characteristics that displayed distinct differences among different city groups classified by dummy variables. One 'X' indicates the possible implications by respective dummy variables.

Table 6.10 concerns the possible determinants in the 1985 model. Several observations are in order regarding the correlation matrix of factual variables. First, RETAILVAL is closely related with OUTPUT and URBANPOP, the coefficients are +0.92 and +0.88, respectively. Therefore, the presence of RETAILVAL in the model also implies the presence of the impact of the size of an economy, not just the size of the local market.

Second, the presence of SEZPOLICY and DSADJACEN also entails the impact of a large amount of accumulated foreign direct investment, better infrastructure, and higher levels of consumption can have on inducing foreign direct investment. Higher

107

levels of private and informal economic sectors are also implied by the four dummy variables. Its impact on inducing foreign direct investment is doubtful despite its significant spatial variation. Nineteen eighty-four was still an early year in China's economic reform and open door policy and the percentage of the private economic sector was still small (1.54 per cent nationally, 2.64 per cent for COC cities, and 19.71 per cent for the SEZs). It is also worth mentioning that although there were differences between SEZs and the rest in urban population size, it did not work to the advantage of SEZs, as the average size of SEZs was still the smallest compared to other groups of cities. At that time, two out of four SEZs, Shenzhen and Zhuhai, were only in their sixth year as cities growing out of two small villages. This no doubt strengthens our belief that SEZ policy did exert significant positive impact on the concentration of foreign direct investment in SEZs.

Third, the negative impact of MP (market potential) should not be interpreted as foreign investors preferring a location farther away rather than closer to the center of a regional market. The negative sign only proves that foreign direct investment was heavily concentrated in Guangdong and Fujian Province and large provinces such as Jiangsu, Sichuan, and Henan, etc. did not get their fair share. The market potential index is calculated in favor of the cities in large provinces such as Jiangsu and Sichuan. These provinces are also geographically in either the north or inland areas of China.

Fourth, having explained the impact of population size, the proportion of the private sector in an economy, and market potential, it is possible to conclude that the presence of COCPOLICY in the model simply conveys the effect that COC policy had on the location of foreign direct investment. DCINLAND just represents the negative effect of the difficulty to interact with home countries on the inflow of foreign direct investment. Less advanced infrastructure in inland provinces enhances this effect. RCENTER (being a large urban center), however, besides its intangible advantages, also had a higher level of industrialization (OUTPUT%) and tax and profit ability (TAXWELL).

Fifth, labor cost, one of the most frequently mentioned determinants in foreign direct investment literature, was not a determinant in the model. Finally, all these conclusions are confirmed by the negative effect of being an inland location. An inland location means not only a smaller size measured in OUTPUT, retail value, and urban population, but also less developed urban infrastructure.

Based on the above analysis, it can be concluded that there were more factors influencing the spatial location of foreign direct investment in 1985 beyond what was revealed in the model. These factors are the conditions of the infrastructure, the amount of accumulated foreign direct investment, and the higher level of industrialization. In summary, the following can be said about the location of foreign direct investment pledged in 1985:

1   City size measured in retail value is the most important explanatory variable. It entails not only the physical size (urban population) of a city, but also the level of consumption of the population. The positive impact of a

Table 6.11
The possible determinants in the location model for 1990

	RETAIL-VAL	SEZ-POLICY	COC-POLICY	COR-POLICY	RCENTER	MP (-)	VAL-ADD%(-)
URBANPOP		*(4)	*(1)	*(2)	*		
RETAILVAL	XX	*(4)	*(1)	*(2)	*		
OUTPUT		*(4)	*(1)	*(2)	*		
MP84		*(3)	*(2)	*(1)	*	XX	
FDISUM		X(1)	X(2)	*(4)			
AVERETAIL		X(1)					
AVEWOKOUT		X(1)					
WAGE		X(1)					
AVEPIPE		X(1)	X(2)	X(2)	X		
URBANPOP%		X(1)	X(2)	*(4)			
OUTPUT%					X		
VALADD%		*(4)	*(3)	*(2)			XX
RESIDOUT%		X(1)	X(2)	X(3)			
RATEOUT		X(1)	X(2)	X(3)			
RATERETL					X		

1. Refer to Table 6.10 for explanation of symbols.
2. The numbers in the parenthesis in SEZPOLICY, COCPOLICY, and CORPOLICY columns are the orders of measurements when four groups of city compared together (including no-special policy city group).
3. The sign in the parenthesis is the sign of coefficient.

109

strong established manufacturing industry is also implied, as there is a strong correlation between a city's total retail value and the size of its economy.

2   The spatial variation of preferential treatments toward foreign direct investment also has important bearing on the spatial pattern of foreign direct investment commitment.

3   The impact of accumulated foreign direct investment on subsequent foreign direct investment inflow should not be ignored though FDISUM is not included in the statistical model. This also applies to the condition of urban infrastructure.

Table 6.11 is comparable to Table 6.10. It shows the locational determinants for foreign direct investment committed in 1990. There are three interval variables and four dummy variables in the model. The dependent variable (the logarithm of foreign direct investment committed in 1990) is regressed against the independent variables having 1986 urban statistics. Compared with 1984, there were more aspects with distinct spatial variation among various city groups. In other words, the divergence among cities increased. This is especially true between SEZ and COC cities on one hand and the rest of the cities on the other. However, it would be improper to state that all these aspects with significant spatial variation implied by the dummy variables have distinct bearings on the dependent variable. The nature and relationships of these aspects need to be further examined.

First, just as in 1984, strong positive relationships existed among RETAILVAL, OUTPUT, and URBANPOP in 1986 (the correlation between RETAILVAL and OUTPUT and that between RETAILVAL and URBANPOP are +0.88 and +0.83, respectively). The inclusion of RETAILVAL as a locational determinant in the 1990 model also implies the impact of the scale of existing manufacturing industry.

Second, strong relationships also exist among another group of variables that includes the rate of industrial growth (RATEOUT), the residual sector in manufacturing industry, i.e. the percentage of those sectors other than state or collectively owned within manufacturing industry (RESIDOUT%), and the processing level of manufacturing industry (VALADD%). The growth rate of manufacturing industry (RATEOUT) during 1984 to 1986 had a strong and positive relationship (+0.61) with RESIDOUT% and a negative relationship (-0.64) with VALADD%. These relationships simply state that the residual economic sector inspired by China's economic reform had a lower level of processing, yet were the driving force behind the growth of manufacturing industry. Cities with predominantly state and collectively owned industries were disadvantaged in the process of economic reform and slow in promoting their growth, although the state and collectively owned industries had the best technological infrastructure. If foreign direct investment was responsive to a more dynamic economic environment, the statistical relationship is most likely to be the negative one between VALADD% and pledged foreign direct investment. That is what appears in the 1990 model. The minus sign of the coefficient of VALADD% should not be interpreted as foreign investors' antipathy toward a more developed

Table 6.12
Possible determinants of location model of 1992 to 1993[1]

	RETAIL-VAL	RATERETL	RCENTER	COCPOLICY	CORPOLICY	TAXWELL
URBANPOP			*	*(1)	*(2)	
RETAILVAL	XX		*	*(1)	*(2)	
OUTPUT			*	*	*	
MP91			*	*(3)	*(2)	
FDISUM			X	X(2)	*(4)	
AVERETAIL			X			
AVEWOKOUT			X			
WAGE			X	X(2)	X(3)	
AVEPIPE				X(2)	X(3)	
TAXWELL						XX
URBANPOP%				X(2)	*(4)	
OUTPUT%			X			
VALADD%						
RESIDOUT%				X(2)	X(2)	
RATERETL		XX				

1. Refer Table 6.11 for symbol explanation.

111

economy. Rather, in China's circumstance, it represents foreign investors' locational preference toward a growing and more dynamic region. Following this reasoning, it is logical to conclude that the advantages that SEZs, COC and COR cities have in higher rates of economic growth and higher percentages of private and informal sectors are reflected by the interval variable VALADD% in the model. Significant differences also existed between the labor cost in SEZs and that of other cities. Yet, the perceivable negative effect that higher labor cost may have been canceled by a higher level of labor productivity.

The above paragraph of analysis enables us to narrow down the possible effects embodied in the policy variables. For SEZPOLICY and COCPOLICY, besides the effect of preferential treatment toward foreign direct investment, the effect of accumulated foreign direct investment, better infrastructure, and higher levels of urbanization are also implied. For the CORPOLICY variable, the only implication other than the designated special policy in COR cities is the positive effect of a better infrastructure.

The advantages of locating in a national or regional urban center in 1986 did not deviate much from 1984. Faster growth rates of retail markets was added to the list of better infrastructure and higher levels of industrialization, in addition to the intangible advantages large urban centers have. The interpretation of market potential is the same as in the 1985 model. Only this time its unique contribution is reduced to two per cent. The spatial pattern of foreign direct investment commitment is less tilted against the spatial pattern of market potential.

Based on these observations, the following statements are appropriate for describing the location of foreign direct investment commitment made in 1990:

1   City size, level of consumption, and the size of economic activity are still the most important locational determinants of foreign direct investment.

2   Foreign direct investment responded to the whole range of incentives available. In 1985, only SEZ and COC policy emerged as possible determinants, although the whole range of preferential treatments was in place. The direct implication for the spatial distribution of foreign direct investment was the spatial expansion of foreign direct investment location and reduction of concentration of foreign direct investment in certain locations. The effect of larger amounts of accumulated foreign direct investment and better infrastructure was still in place.

3   Higher economic growth rates were also relevant to foreign investors' location decision making. A faster growing economy and a more dynamic economic environment provided by a large percentage of the private sector were welcomed by foreign investors.

4   The impact of being a national or regional urban center persisted. The sources of this impact in the 1990 location model come from higher growth rates of markets, higher level of industrialization, and better infrastructure.

112

The reinterpretation of the 1992 to 1993 model is based on Table 6.12. It summarizes the locational determinants for the foreign direct investment committed during 1992 to 1993. The statistical model includes six independent variables, and one-half of them are interval variables. The implications of the dummy variables can be elaborated as follows.

The implication embodied in RCENTER other than some intangible effects includes higher market potential, higher levels of consumption, and higher levels of accumulated foreign direct investment. The advantage of large urban centers over other cities in infrastructure was no longer significant. The attractiveness that higher labor productivity could have been canceled by higher labor cost.

The inclusion of COCPOLICY implies that other than the incentives, foreign investors might also have responded to COCs' larger amounts of accumulated foreign direct investment, higher market potential, higher levels of urbanization, better infrastructure, and a more dynamic economic environment. Compared with COCPOLICY, the urbanization and accumulated foreign direct investment effect are absent in the implication of CORPOLICY.

By looking at these three dummy variables simultaneously, we find that both higher market potential and higher labor cost are implied by all three variables. The implication of the positive effect of market potential suggests the deviation of the 1992 to 1993 model from the 1990 model. As one remembers, it has a negative relationship with the dependent variable in previous models.

The common implication of higher labor cost by the three dummy variables reveals that higher labor cost was not a significant deterring factor in inducing foreign direct investment. While higher labor cost was evened out by higher productivity in large urban centers, there is no evidence to show that COC and COR cities in 1991 retained higher levels of labor productivity. There is no doubt that since 1991 the locational pattern of foreign direct investment commitment started to deviate from previous patterns in a significant way. Namely, foreign direct investment started to spread in a way that the concentration of foreign direct investment in SEZs is no longer significant to the overall location pattern. The special policies gave way to cities' built-up merits. With the above analysis on the implication of dummy variables and the preliminary conclusion on the 1992 to 1993 locational model, a more concise interpretation of the model is warranted:

1   the location pattern of foreign direct investment enters a mature stage within which foreign direct investment is responsive to the true merit of a location, rather than government imposed advantages such as incentives and preferential policy. The merits that matter most, the major locational determinants of foreign direct investment, are the major aspects of the local market. These aspects include the size, growth rate, and its potential for ease of access to other regional markets.

2   The replacement of SEZPOLICY by RATERETL suggests the cessation of the spell that SEZs had on investors and the commencement of the spatial spread of foreign direct investment. While other special policies (COC and

113

COR policy) were still relevant, their importance was much less than in previous years. The fact that RCENTER holds a more important position in the model strongly suggests that the spread of foreign direct investment was lead by major regional urban centers across the country, not just along the coastal provinces, as all the major preferential policies were conferred to coastal cities in this analysis.

3   Urban infrastructure and a dynamic economic environment are implied by the three dummy variables. Labor cost was implied to be irrelevant (or a deterrent) to the location of foreign direct investment.

4   Unlike the 1985 and 1990 models, the accumulated foreign direct investment joined the group of size variables (OUTPUT, URBANPOP, RETAILVAL) in the 1992 to 1993 model. The correlations between RETAILVAL and OUTPUT, URBANPOP, and FDISUM are +0.93, +0.91, and +0.73 respectively. As such, the inclusion of RETAILVAL in the model alone makes it possible to infer that the scale of industrial activity, city size, level of consumption, and accumulated foreign direct investment all have an important bearing on the location decision of foreign investors.

The major locational determinants of foreign direct investment in China, 1979 to 1993

After analysis of the locational model at different times and a detailed discussion of typical models, some conclusion can be made as to the overall locational determinants of foreign direct investment commitment since 1979. Overall, models change over the years, yet not without consistency. Foreign direct investment committed in China diffused, especially after 1991, and the locational determinants reflected the merits of a location rather than government imposed policy instruments.

Aspects of city size (mostly the size of the local market, sometimes the urban population) were the most important explanatory factor in the location of foreign direct investment. In the early years, it was just the size and level of consumption (together they determine the size of the local market). Starting in 1992, aspects such as the growth rate of the local market and the market potential also became important locational determinants. Before turning to other characteristics of the overall location pattern, it is important to differentiate between the meaning of the market in this analysis with that used within the context of the location of foreign direct investment among countries. One city's market is in no way as segmented as national markets. While national market size affects foreign direct investment by affecting the volume of sales and economies of scale of international production, a city's market affects the location of foreign direct investment more by the benefit brought with the size of a city. The size benefit includes not only the volume of sales, but also the economies of agglomeration of population and economic activity. This is the reason market is

114

called local market size most of the time or just city size reflected with level of consumption.

Second, policy instruments do have an impact on the location of foreign direct investment at a subnational level, especially in the earlier stages of foreign direct investment involvement in a specific host country. The fact that most of the foreign direct investment committed during the first few years in China was concentrated in the SEZs, especially Shenzhen, cannot be explained otherwise. The impact of SEZ policy on the overall locational pattern of foreign direct investment commitment lingered until 1991. The impact of special policy and preferential treatments toward foreign direct investment can be intensified if foreign investors encounter a dissimilar social, economic, and legal system. The decreasing impact of policy instruments also shows the experience effect on foreign investors as a whole. As foreign investors grow more comfortable and confident about China's economic and social systems, they start to venture away from areas with special policy status.

The relevance of distance from home country in terms of both social and physical distances is also proven. This is especially true in the earlier stages of foreign direct investment commitment. Before 1989, the closeness that cities in Guangdong and Fujian Provinces possessed had put them in an advantageous position in receiving the inflow of foreign direct investment from Hong Kong and Macau. The evidence of the relevance of distance indirectly measured by cities' location with reference to the sea is sporadic. The disadvantages of inland locations may be manifested in ways such as no special open door policy and less developed urban infrastructure.

The advantages of an urban center are always relevant to the location decisions of foreign investors. These advantages may be manifested in some specific locational attribute as well as some intangible advantages associated with large national and regional urban centers. The consistent relevancy and increasing importance at later years when foreign direct investment spread to broader geographic regions suggest that large cities lead the way of spatial expansion of foreign direct investment.

Although they are not included in the factual variable models, the impact of experience, the economies of agglomeration, a better infrastructure, and a dynamic growing economy are strongly implied. The impact was embodied in various policy, distance, or locational dummy variables. In the 1992 to 1993 model, the accumulation effect of foreign direct investment due to existing foreign direct investment is implied by an interval variable, the size of the local market. Also, implied in the models is the irrelevancy of labor cost overall as a locational determinant. It was either not considered at all or was discarded after being evaluated against other variables. The first possibility is very high considering that the overall labor cost is much lower compared with that in home countries.

In understanding the locational determinants of foreign direct investment committed during 1985 to 1993, it is important to point out that the model changes over the years reflect the dynamic nature of the location of foreign direct investment within a subnational context. The changes in the spatial distribution of foreign direct investment can be interpreted as the result of a dynamic process brought out by three forces. The first one is the changing nature of foreign direct investment itself. The second is the self-evolving process of local economic and social systems that changes

115

the spatial form of locational specific advantages among regions. The third source is the changes of investment environment, opportunities, and industrial structure (in terms of structure of firms, firm behavior, and market results) induced by foreign direct investment in the last period. Two examples are the positive experience effect and the effect of the market and operational efficiency induced by the agglomeration of foreign direct investment. The experience effect may encourage subsequential investment and new investors to venture to new locations; the economies of agglomeration of foreign direct investment may lead foreign direct investment to continue to cluster in certain regions. Yet, the continuing concentration of foreign direct investment in certain locations may also lead to the diminishing of investment opportunities, declining marginal profit, and increasing competition, that will eventually lead to the spatial spread of foreign direct investment. The spatial spread of the distribution of foreign direct investment in China was most probably the result of impacts from all of the three sources.

Effectiveness of models: latent and factual variable models compared

First, it is obvious that regression analyses using latent variables are far more parsimonious than those using factual locational variables. Second, models using latent variables are more concise and stable in a sense that the independent variables are close to being independent (latent variables are obtained by factor analysis using the orthogonal rotation method). One can separate the contribution of each latent variable. This is not true for factual variable models. It is tempting to explain the impact of each variable according to their coefficients. Yet because of the correlation between variables, one cannot pinpoint exactly how important each variable is. The impact of one variable is dependent upon others in the models.

The application of these two approaches to the model building of this research reveals other interesting aspects. By comparing the summary results of models using latent variables with those using factual locational variables, one can detect that latent variable models do not do as well as factual variable models before 1989 concerning explained variance. Starting from 1990, however, the effectiveness of these two approaches started to converge. It is possible that if more recent data were added into this analysis, the latent variable model would surpass the factual variable model in effectiveness. The possible explanation may lie in changes in the locational mechanism of foreign direct investment itself. At the earlier stage of foreign direct investment involvement in China, the locational decision making of foreign investors was simply based on a limited number of factors because of limited information inputs. These factors most likely do not reflect the fundamental characteristics of the city system. Rather, these factors may reflect the idiosyncrasy of foreign investors based on limited information on the locational attributes of available location choices. As such, a correctly specified factual variable model may do a better job than a latent variable model. At later stages, as foreign direct investment diversified and foreign investors became more informed, locational decision making became more rational

116

and was incorporated with more locational attributes, the latent variable model would reflect the locational pattern of foreign direct investment.

Another aspect is that the latent variable model stays much more stable than the factual variable model. With only several latent variables, there are no misgivings in the possible exclusion of relevant variables in model building. Yet, it is exactly here that the weakness of the latent variable model lies. One cannot test specific hypotheses or the impact of specific locational variables. The latent variable model may be more appropriate for predicting, while the explicit variable model is more appropriate for confirmation and explanation.

Notes

1   These small capital phrases are used to denote a latent variable (factor).
2   Actually the COCPOLICY variable does not surface in 1989 model. The reason for the assertion is that COCPOLICY is closely related to DCPORT which refers to whether a city is a port city. As indicated in Chapter Four, COCPOLICY cities are just 14 port cities starting from the top of list in terms of population size, and size of economic activity.

7 The country of origin effect

Introduction

There is an important assumption in the analysis of the general pattern of foreign direct investment in China. It is the homogeneity of foreign direct investment as opposed to investment made by indigenous firms. As elaborated in the conceptual framework, foreign direct investment is far more diverse. Foreign direct investment in a host country may consist of investments from different home countries, encompassing a wide range of economic activity, and be of different types for the strategies adopted by foreign investors. All the characteristics accompanied with different types of investment may have important implications on their location patterns. This chapter intends to look into one aspect of this diversity: the impact of different home countries.

The data used in this chapter's analysis is the combination of the firm database and city database. For the location modeling, data on the dependent variable is the accumulated amount of registered capital of foreign invested ventures from 1979 to 1987. Data of independent variables are from the 1986 urban statistics. Only the major investors, namely Hong Kong, the US, Japan, European countries[1] as a whole, and Singapore, are singled out for the location modeling.

This chapter proceeds in several steps. First, the spatial patterns of the presence of foreign direct investment from each home country are discussed, followed by the statistical modeling of the spatial variation of foreign direct investment for these investors. Finally, the differences in locational patterns among different countries are analyzed within the context of foreign direct investment characteristics. The locational model building uses the same set of independent variables as in the last chapter.

The spatial patterns of the presence of foreign direct investment from major home countries

Table 7.1 shows the different saturation rates of the major investors. It appears that all investors from different counties were responsive to special policies toward foreign direct investment. From cities with special economic zone policy to cities with no special policy the saturation rates decrease for all five areas. The differences among countries, however, are shown in two aspects. First, investment from Hong Kong was much more pervasive than investment from other countries. While only a little more than 20 per cent of the non-special policy cities were left without Hong Kong investment, this measure was approximately 67 per cent and 79 per cent for the US and Japan, respectively. On top of that, one-half of the CORs (coastal open regions) were void of both US and Japanese investment. This suggests that the presence of US investment (Japanese investment to a much lesser degree) was less affected by preferential policy than Hong Kong investment.

Table 7.2 shows different countries' preferences with respect to city locations. Again, differences among countries emerge. While Hong Kong investment again is more prevalent, its presence from coast to periphery descends accordingly. Investment from Singapore displays the same pattern. While overall this is also true for foreign direct investment from the US, Japan, and Europe, foreign direct investment from these countries deviates from Hong Kong's pattern in their higher saturation rates in peripheral regions than those in inland regions. This little difference should not be overlooked because it may show the difference of firm types and strategies between NICs on the one side and developed countries on the other.

As to country differences in their presence in different sizes of cities, the grouping of home countries changes a little. From Table 7.3, one can see that investment from developed countries again shows a propensity toward national and large regional urban and manufacturing centers. The differences between the saturation rates of local urban centers and those of small cities are negligible. Hong Kong investment again is more pervasive as there is little difference between the saturation rates of different groups. Nonetheless, the preference toward larger cities is clearly shown.

The above observation is largely confirmed by a logistic regression modeling of the presence of foreign direct investment from different countries.[2] What this modeling shows is how a host of location specific variables can affect the odds of a city becoming a foreign direct investment recipient city. The odds here are the ratio of the probability of being a foreign direct investment recipient city to the probability of not being a foreign direct investment recipient city. A linear relationship is assumed between the log of the odds, the dependent variable, and the independent location specific variables.

Tables 7.4 through Table 7.8 show the statistical modeling for each major home country. β is the coefficient for each variable, Wald and significance levels are used to test the hypothesis that the coefficient of a variable is zero. r shows the linear correlation between the dependent and independent variable. Exp(β) shows how much the odds will change with a unit of change in the independent variable.

Table 7.1

Presence rate of foreign direct investment from different home country in city groups of different special policy towards foreign direct investment

	SEZ policy cities	COC policy cities	COR policy cities	Cities with no preferential policy
Hong Kong	1.00	1.00	1.00	0.78
United States	0.75	1.00	0.51	0.33
Japan	1.00	1.00	0.45	0.21
Europe	0.50	0.85	0.28	0.11
Singapore	1.00	0.77	0.38	0.19
Number of cities	4	13	29	103

Table 7.2

Presence rate of foreign direct investment from different home countries in city groups of different location (from coast to periphery)

	Coastal port cities	Coastal cities	Inland cities	Periphery cities
Hong Kong	1.00	0.93	0.79	0.67
United States	0.88	0.48	0.28	0.38
Japan	0.82	0.40	0.19	0.25
EC	0.65	0.22	0.09	0.17
Singapore	0.59	0.38	0.19	0.17
Number of cities	17	55	53	24

As shown in Table 7.4, it seems that only the size of the local market is statistically significant in being able to change the odds for the presence of Hong Kong investment. These results should be considered contradictory to the observations made by simply looking at the saturation rates. One should be reminded that this statistical conclusion results from treating total foreign direct investment realized during the years 1979 to 1987 as if it occurred at a single point in time. It would be unrealistic to exclude the importance of other urban characteristics in affecting Hong Kong investors' decisions. It has been established in Chapter Five that the characteristics that separate a recipient city from a foreign direct investment void city can change over time.

If we conclude that only local market size was statistically significant in changing a city's odds to receive any Hong Kong investment during the years 1979 to 1987 as a whole, the same cannot be said about other major investors. The US, Japan, and European countries seem to have similar patterns (Table 7.5 to Table 7.7). Besides local market size, being a COC (coastal open city) could also increase the odds of accommodating investment from the US, Japan, and European countries. The

Table 7.3
Presence rate of foreign direct investment by home country and by cities of different sizes*

	National urban centers	Regional urban centers	Local urban centers	Small cities
Hong Kong	1.00	1.00	0.97	0.80
United States	1.00	1.00	0.41	0.39
Japan	1.00	0.88	0.31	0.30
European Community	1.00	1.00	0.28	0.12
Singapore	1.00	0.38	0.24	0.29
Number of cities	3	8	29	109

* Levels of city size are determined by both urban population (URBANPOP) size and scale of industrial activity, and gross industrial output (OUTPUT). To be a national center, a city must have over three million URBANPOP and have over 300 million RMB OUTPUT. Other levels of cities conform with the following combined criteria of URBANPOP and OUTPUT: one to three million and over 90 million RMB, one-half to one million and over 30 million RMB, and less than one-half million and less than 30 million RMB.

Table 7.4
Logistic regression model for the presence of Hong Kong investment

Variable	β and standard error	Wald and significance	r	Exp(β)
RETAILVAL	3.38E-05, 8.13E-06	17.21, 0.00	0.34	1.00
Constant	-2.02, 0.70	8.34, 0.00	-	-

Table 7.5
Logistic regression model for the presence of US investment

Variable	β and standard error	Wald and significance	r	Exp(β)
RETAILVAL	7.75E-06, 2.21E-06	12.28, 0.00	0.22	1.00
AVERETAIL	0.51, 0.12	16.68, 0.00	0.27	1.67
COCPOLICY*	9.19, 26.14	0.12, 0.73	0.00	9782.13
Constant	-4.71, 0.82	32.90, 0.00		

* The small Wald statistic and high significance level of this variable is caused by disadvantages inherent in the Wald statistic when its β value and standard deviation of β are large. A test of modeling without COCPOLICY proves that this variable is actually significant.

Table 7.6
Logistic regression model for the presence of Japanese investment

Variable	β and standard error	Wald and significance	r	Exp(β)
RETAILVAL	7.36E-06, 7.73E-06	18.23, 0.00	0.29	1.00
COCPOLICY*	8.42, 16.75	0.25, 0.62	0.00	4539.58
Constant	-2.32, 0.40	34.41,0.00	-	-

* As in Table 7.5, this variable is proved to be significant in the model.

Table 7.7
Logistic regression model for the presence of European investment

Variable	β and standard error	Wald and significance	r	Exp(β)
RETAILVAL	9.36E-06, 2.24E-06	17.44, 0.00	0.32	1.00
COCPOLICY	2.84, 0.95	8.90, 0.00	0.21	17.10
RCENTER*	9.37, 3.98	0.09, 0.76	0.00	11764.86
Constant	-4.06, 0.64	4.86, 0.00	-	-

* RCENTER is significant in the model.

differences among those countries, though, are that the level of consumption also mattered to foreign direct investment from the US, and being a national or a regional urban center to foreign direct investment from West European countries.

One should be reminded that while COCPOLICY is designed primarily to reflect one special kind of open door policy in China, it also shares much in common in its content with another location variable, DCPORT which represents the port cities at the prefecture level or above. As such, the importance of COC policy in increasing a city's odds of being a foreign direct investment recipient city can also be extended to being a coastal port city. In other words, being a coastal port city could also increase a city's odds of being considered as a possible locational choice of foreign direct investment. This extended explanation is not just playing with the definition and design of variables. It is very much in line with the observations based on the saturation rates of foreign direct investment presence. It was shown that the saturation rates of the presence for all home countries decrease with the increasing distance from China's coast.

The presence of Singapore investment stands as a separate category. It seems that a city's distance from home countries (as referred to Hong Kong, Macau, Singapore, and overseas Chinese investors) mattered a great deal. Variables that could increase a city's odds also included the size of the local market and the level of industrialization.

Based on the above observations, it can be concluded that there is much in common among different home countries in choosing the kinds of cities as possible locational choices for their investment. Both saturation rates and logistic regression analyses show that among other urban characteristics, a city's status about whether to retain special policy, distances from home countries, and its size are the most important variables in determining its odds as a possible location for foreign investment.

Table 7.8
Logistic regression model for the presence of Singapore investment

Variable	β and standard error	Wald and significance	r	Exp(β)
RETAILVAL	4.65E-06, 1.50E-06	9.68, 0.00	0.21	1.00
DSADJACEN	3.34, 1.12	8.79, 0.00	0.19	28.21
DSCLOSE	5.02, 1.65	9.23, 0.00	0.20	152.29
AVEOUTPUT	0.04, 0.01	5.89, 0.02	0.15	1.03
Constant	-5.20, 1.31	15.71, 0.00	-	-

Apart from the common features, the differences among countries are just as important. Pattern differences are identified between two groups of home countries. One includes developed countries, another includes newly industrializing countries (Hong Kong and Singapore). The differences between the two arise from the nature of their distances with potential host cities. In general, as there are no special social ties shared between developed countries with a group of cities in China. Foreign investors from these countries marked the ease of interaction with parent companies in home countries an important criterion in screening cities as possible locational choices. For Hong Kong and Singapore, they have strong social ties, thus, the shortest social and psychic distance, with two of the provinces in China, namely Guangdong and Fujian Province. This social distance coincides with geographical distance. As a result, investors from both Hong Kong and Singapore are most likely to choose cities in Guangdong and Fujian Province as their possible locational choices. One might argue that there are large differences between Hong Kong and Singapore as shown in their logistic regression models. It is in these authors' opinion that the difference only proves there was a lag between Singapore investment and Hong Kong investment. Hong Kong investors went to mainland China first. Their experience of investing in mainland China and the sheer volume of their total investment made their presence during 1979 to 1987 statistically insensitive to the host-home distance factor. In the earlier years of China's opening, the presence of Hong Kong investment could show the same pattern as Singapore shown in Table 7.7, which is already established to an extent in Chapter Four.

Statistical location models for different home countries

Having discussed what in general makes foreign investors not choose certain cities as their possible locational choices, we turn to find out what factors usually determine which cities get more foreign direct investment. Statistical models are built for each of the major investors, and their differences are compared (see Tables 7.9 to 7.13).

Foreign direct investment characteristics of different home countries and location patterns

Apart from the interval nature of the variables in the American, Japanese, and European models, all three models have RETAILVAL as the most important explanatory variable. It contributes 0.26, 0.30, and 0.39 to the r^2 in the US, Japan, and Europe models, respectively. The US model seems different from the Japanese and European models in that it has AVEPIPE (infrastructure measurement) as its second important variable rather than AVERETAIL (level of consumption). In truth, this difference is only superficial because the relationship between AVEPIPE and AVERETAIL is very strong (correlation coefficient is 0.72) in US invested cities. As for the cities with European investment, the correlation between the two variables is 0.81. These suggest one thing: that there is no significant difference among the American, Japanese, and European models. Rather, investment from these developed

Table 7.9

Location pattern of foreign direct investment from Hong Kong

Dependent variable	log of registered capital of Hong Kong invested ventures from 1978 to 1987
r^2	0.54
Degrees of freedom	119
Constant, standard error, t, and significance	2.10, 0.10, 2.59, 0.00
F value and significance	28.63, 0.00
K-S statistic and significance	0.07, >0.20

Independent variables	Cumulative r squared	Coefficient and standard error	Beta	Tolerance level	t value and significance
RETAILVAL	0.22	1.46E-06, 2.44E-07	0.39	0.90	5.99, 0.00
DSADJACEN	0.40	1.41, 0.24	0.39	0.85	5.80, 0.00
DSCLOSE	0.48	1.00, 0.28	0.23	0.92	3.52, 0.00
AVERETAIL	0.51	0.04, 0.01	0.20	0.79	2.93, 0.00
DCPORT	0.54	0.54, 0.19	0.19	0.92	2.90, 0.00
RCENTER	0.55	0.50, 0.24	0.13	0.95	2.06, 0.04

Table 7.10
Location pattern of foreign direct investment from Singapore

Dependent variable	log of registered capital of Singapore invested ventures from 1978 to 1987
r^2	0.47
Degrees of freedom	41
Constant, standard error, t, and significance	1.89, 0.12, 2.06, 0.00
F value, significance	11.93, 0.00
K-S statistic, significance	0.085, >0.20

Independent variables	Cumulative r squared	Coefficient and standard error	Beta	Tolerance level	t value and significance
RETAILVAL	0.23	9.66E-07, 2.20E-07	0.50	0.99	4.38, 0.00
SEZPOLICY	0.41	1.15, 0.29	0.46	0.97	4.05, 0.00
COCPOLICY	0.47	0.44, 0.21	0.24	0.97	2.06, 0.04

Table 7.11
Location pattern of foreign direct investment from US

Dependent variable	log of registered capital of US invested ventures from 1978 to 1987
r^2	0.43
Degrees of freedom	62
Constant, standard error, t, and significance	1.29, 0.23, 5.62, 0.00
F value, significance	15.45, 0.00
K-S statistic, significance	0.071, >0.20

Independent variables	Cumulative r squared	Coefficient and standard error	Beta	Tolerance level	t value and significance
RETAILVAL	0.26	1.24E-06, 2.68E-07	0.45	0.97	4.64, 0.00
AVEPIPE	0.39	17.04, 4.66	0.35	0.99	3.66, 0.00
AVEWOKOUT	0.43	0.006, 0.003	0.20	0.98	2.10, 0.04

Table 7.12
Location pattern of foreign direct investment from Japan

Dependent variable	registered capital of Japan invested ventures	
r^2	0.48	
Degrees of Freedom	48	
Constant, standard error, t, and significance	1.98, 0.14, 13.79, 0.00	
F value, significance	14.98, 0.00	
K-S statistic, significance	0.14, 0.02	

Independent variables	Cumulative r squared	Coefficient and standard error	Beta	Tolerance level	t value and significance
RETAILVAL	0.30	9.66E-07, 2.35E-07	0.44	0.94	4.11, 0.00
AVERETAIL	0.41	0.03, 0.01	0.30	0.94	2.83, 0.00
DCINLAND	0.48	-0.51, 0.20	-0.27	0.96	-2.56, 0.01

Table 7.13

Location pattern of foreign direct investment from European countries

Dependent variable	log of registered capital of W. Europe invested ventures from 1978 to 1987	
r^2	0.62	
Degrees of freedom	29	
Constant, standard error, t, and significance	1.77, 0.16, 11.16, 0.00	
F value, significance	24.01, 0.00	
K-S statistic, significance	0.07, >0.20	

Independent Variables	Cumulative r squared	Coefficient and standard error	Beta	Tolerance Level	t value and significance
RETAILVAL	0.39	1.09E-06, 2.32E-07	0.54	0.97	4.70, 0.00
AVERETAIL	0.62	0.04, 0.01	0.49	0.97	4.21, 0.00

131

countries was predominantly affected by one factor, the local market. This local market factor is reflected by two market variables: RETAILVAL and AVERETAIL, with the first one focusing on the size of the market and the latter on the level of consumption of the market. With the strong correlation between the level of consumption and condition of the local infrastructure, we may include the infrastructure as a factor in determining the location of investment from developed countries.

The minor difference between these three models is reflected in the third variable that appeared in the American and Japanese models (there is no third variable in the European model). For the US model, the third variable is labor productivity (AVEWOKOUT) and DCINLAND for the Japan model.

One common aspect that exists among these developed countries and is not reflected explicitly in their models is their preference for the three national urban and manufacturing centers, namely Beijing, Shanghai, and Tianjin. This assertion is based on the strong correlation between the dependent variable and NCENTER that is a dummy variable representing these three cities. The lack of explicit representation in their statistical models is attributed to the strong correlation between NCENTER and RETAILVAL.

Location model for foreign direct investment from Hong Kong and Singapore

It is evident from the last section that there are major differences between foreign direct investment location patterns of developed countries and those of Hong Kong and Singapore, two city NICs that happen to have close social ties with China. Their differences can be summarized as follows. The social and physical distance factor from Hong Kong played a prominent role in the spatial distribution of Hong Kong investment. For Singaporean investment, the major factor was the special policy. For the investment from developed countries, however, the major locational determinant was the local market factor that included both the size and the level of the consumption aspects of the local market. The framework laid out in Chapter Four suggests that foreign direct investment of different characteristics may respond to different sets of location specific advantages of host regions (cities).

The deviation of location patterns among different home countries can be attributed to several aspects of foreign direct investment characteristics associated with home countries. Based on our locational framework, these aspects may include:

1   industry-mix;

2   ownership specific advantages due to firm size, current stage of firms' life cycle, and/or position in a production process;

3   social and physical distance between host regions and home countries; and

4   all the other relevant factors.

Since the location patterns of different home countries can be grouped into country groups such as newly industrializing countries and developed countries, it is only logical to try to put the major investors in groups according to the characteristics of their foreign direct investment and then compare the groupings. The foreign direct investment characteristics are reflected in these aspects as mentioned in the last paragraph. If the groupings are similar, then we can elaborate on the foreign direct investment characteristics of different groups of home countries and attribute these characteristics to the source of the deviation of their location patterns.

In grouping the major investors, cluster analysis is used.[3] Cluster analysis refers to a variety of multivariate procedures used to create classifications. A specific clustering method starts with a sample of entities with a host of variables showing their characteristics, attempts to recognize the patterns established by these variables, and classifies the entities into relatively homogeneous groups. The samples of entities in this analysis are the major foreign investors. The variables used to classify these countries are from the firm database.

Three country groups

Table 7.14 shows the results of cluster analysis of the five major home countries. It is obvious that the five countries can be put into three groups: 1) Hong Kong and other countries (represented by Hong Kong), 2) the US, Japan, and European countries (represented by the US), and 3) Singapore. Table 7.15 and Table 7.16 list the major characteristics of different groups. Table 7.17 and Table 7.18 reveal structural characteristics in the manufacturing industry.

It is not surprising to find that the US, Japan, and European countries are in one group and Hong Kong and other countries in another. Singapore stands alone as a separate category. Although it is not a perfect match between this grouping and the one based on location patterns, it nonetheless shows the link between the foreign direct investment characteristics of a country and its location pattern. The following several sections will elaborate on the different foreign direct investment characteristics displayed each country group.

Location patterns and sectoral compositions of foreign direct investment   Table 7.15 and Table 7.17 display the differences in sectoral composition of different home countries. First, we look at the sectoral composition in three sectors: primary, manufacturing, and service sectors. Overall, 56 per cent of investment by the US and other developed country investors is concentrated in manufacturing industry. Singapore registered the lowest percentage of manufacturing investment at 38 per cent. As agricultural investment was small for every country, the reverse of the sequence of comparison in manufacturing industry percentage is true for the service sector. Singapore had the highest percentage, 55 per cent, of investment in the service industry.

If we look into the structure of manufacturing investment, we find that different countries are differentiated from each other even more. Table 7.17 shows the structure of manufacturing industry for each country group. Overall, there are three

133

Table 7.14

Cluster analysis: the agglomeration schedule using average linkage within group

Stage	Clusters combined cluster 1	cluster 2	Coefficient	Stage of cluster first appears cluster 1	cluster 2	Next stage
1	US	Europe	0.28	0	0	2
2	US	Japan	0.06	1	0	4
3	Hong Kong	other countries	0.0030	0	0	5
4	US	Singapore	-0.06	2	0	5
5	Hong Kong	US	-0.19	3	4	0

groups of industries that attracted most of the foreign direct investment during the period 1979 to 1987. These included labor intensive and low technology industries such as food, textiles, rubber and plastic products. The establishment and expansion of these 'foot loose' industries requires little in the way of backward linkages. Rather, they may require efficient operation of forward linkages and services, especially if they are intended for international markets. Another group of industries includes those based on natural resources and materials that are usually available in limited locations. This group of industries only includes stone, clay, and glass products in the analysis. The third group includes machinery, transportation equipment, electric, and electronic industries. The industrial sectors in this group are usually considered technology intensive industries whose development usually requires extensive forward and backward linkages. In other words, existing manufacturing activity can be an important locational determinant. Usually they also have higher requirements of labor. However, at least some industries can also be just labor intensive if only the assembly of standardized semi-products is involved. One example is offshore electronics plants.

Compared with other countries, investment from Hong Kong was more diversified across the industries. However, the three groups of industries still account for 65 per cent of its total investment. Within these three groups though, the first group of industries makes up the most. They account for 34 per cent of total investment from Hong Kong, with textile and leather taking up 19.4 per cent of its total, food taking 8.2 per cent, and rubber and plastic products taking 7.8 per cent. The third group of industries makes up 23 per cent of total Hong Kong investment. Within this group, the electronic industry makes up 13.9 per cent Hong Kong's total. Stone, clay and glass products take 6.4 per cent of its total. Other than these industries, public utilities

Table 7.15
Foreign direct investment characteristics of different home country group

Group	Registered capital (in 1000 US$)	Agricultural sector %	Manufacturing sector %	Service sector %	Average size of venture (in 10,000 US$)	Average duration of venture (year)
Hong Kong	10,640,460	0.08	49.07	50.85	156.18	10
US	3,154,810	0.03	56.65	43.32	362.62	13
Singapore	397,880	7.00	37.95	55.05	213.59	14

Table 7.16
Foreign direct investment characteristics of different country group*

Group	Number of ventures	% CJV	% EJV	% WFV	% Est. by 1983	% Est. in 1984	% Est. in 1985	% Est. in 1986	% Est. in 1987
Hong Kong	6852	49.4	49.1	1.5	5.6	17.0	35.8	17.1	23.9
US	881	16.3	81.6	2.0	5.7	1.8	28.8	27.3	26.4
Singapore	187	25.1	70.1	4.8	2.7	7.5	33.2	26.7	29.4

* The sum of percentages of established in each year may not be exactly 100, as there are about 40 ventures without date of establishment.

Table 7.17
Structure of manufacturing investment of different country group

Industry Sectors	Hong Kong	United States	Singapore
Mining and logging	0.25	0.12	0.00
Food, beverage, tobacco	8.28	16.86	15.48
Textile, apparel, clothing, leather, and leather products	19.42	4.84	1.50
Lumber, furniture, paper, and paper products	4.55	1.55	2.27
Publishing, cultural and artistic products	2.82	1.24	0.39
Electricity and steam	8.81	0.05	0.00
Petroleum and coal processing	2.29	0.06	0.00
Chemical industry	2.43	4.47	3.90
Drug industry	0.29	5.15	0.00
Rubber and plastic products	7.75	3.74	7.47
Stone, clay, and glass products	6.42	9.65	25.16
Primary metal industry	2.22	0.70	1.70
Fabricated and metal products	4.56	1.88	5.54
Machinery industry	2.69	6.59	5.83
Transportation equipments	2.51	20.50	1.28
Electric industry	4.38	1.80	2.17
Electronic industry	13.91	18.24	15.51
Instruments and related products	0.35	2.32	1.13
Others (unclassified)	0.57	0.20	1.01

137

Table 7.18
Similarity of structures of manufacturing investment among different home countries*

	Hong Kong	US	Europe	Japan	Singapore	others
Hong Kong	1	0.41	0.32	0.38	0.64	0.44
US	0.41	1	0.94	0.78	0.50	0.54
Europe	00.32	0.94	1	0.72	0.70	0.38
Japan	00.38	0.78	0.72	1	0.68	0.56
Singapore	00.64	0.50	0.70	0.68	1	0.69
Others	00.44	0.54	0.38	0.56	0.69	1

* The number in each cell is the Spearman rank correlation coefficient.

such as electricity and steam account for the considerable amount of 8.8 per cent. The rest of its investment was spread equally across all other industries.

For investments from Singapore, the percentages taken by the three groups of industries are more than 80 per cent. The stone, clay, and glass products alone account for 25 per cent of Singapore's total. While the first group of industries (food, textile, and rubber and plastic products) made up 32 per cent of its total investment, the third group took 24 per cent in total and was dominated by the electronics industry (15.5 per cent).

Although there is a difference, the distributions of Singapore and Hong Kong manufacturing investment were not different. Primarily, they concentrated on low technology and labor intensive industries. This gives an obvious contrast the investment from developed countries led by the US and Japan. Their investment in the third group of industries (machinery, transportation equipment, electric, and electronic industries) made up more than 47 per cent of their total manufacturing investment, which is twice that for Hong Kong or Singapore. Investment in the first group of industry only took about 25 per cent of their total investment. The percentage for stone, clay, and glass products took close to 10 per cent. Other than their concentration on the third group of industries, developed countries also distinguished themselves by investing 10 per cent of their total investment in chemical and drug industries, another sector that is usually considered technology intensive. The percentages for both Singapore and Hong Kong and other countries were less than four per cent.

Table 7.17 also shows that investments from developed countries were heavily concentrated on the third group of industries. Different countries had different focuses on these relatively high technology sectors. For instance, investment in electronic industry accounts for 46 per cent of the total investment from Japan, and investment in transportation equipment takes up 45 per cent of the total investment from European countries.

These structural differences contributed to the locational differences among country groups. For the investment from Hong Kong and Singapore, because of its labor intensive and low technology nature, it requires little location specific advantages compared with investment from developed countries such as the US, Japan, and Germany. Coupled with their strong social ties with and geographical proximity to Guangdong and Fujian Provinces, there is little wonder why investment from Hong Kong was heavily concentrated in these two provinces. On the contrary, a larger portion of investment from developed countries was of high technology and required many location specific advantages that are usually available in large cities with strong established manufacturing activities.

As a conclusion to this section, it is appropriate to state that the locational requirement of different industries is still part of the explanation in the difference between countries, although international production by multinational enterprises has largely transcended the limitation of local geographical patterns of factors of production. Different countries have different industrial mixes due to home country market conditions and industrial structures, which further induce locational deviation from each other in host countries.

139

Firm specific advantages of different home countries and location patterns

Besides the structural differences of investment, foreign direct investment from different countries can also be identified with different firm specific advantages. Tables 7.15 and 7.16 show just the tip of the iceberg in this respect. Among all the differences between the three country groups, the average size of their venture and the most used mode of entry deserve special attention. On average, ventures invested by investors from the US and other developed countries are twice the size of those by investors from Hong Kong and other developing countries. With larger size and perhaps more established ownership-specific advantages at stake, investors from developed countries choose equity joint ventures (EJVs) as the dominant entry mode. Hong Kong investors, by contrast, assigned great importance to cooperative joint ventures (CJVs), especially in the earlier years during the period between 1979 and 1987. There were as many CJVs as EJVs during the whole period.

With varying sizes of investment, different entry modes, and different firm specific advantages, investors from different home countries were not committed at the same level. This is evidenced in part by the duration of ventures, with Hong Kong invested ventures having the shortest term of project duration.

The structural comparison of when and what portions of ventures were established during 1979 to 1987 is also indicative of the different characteristics among investors from different home countries. Special attention should be paid to three years: 1985, 1986, and 1987. Within the 1985 booming year, all the countries established 29 per cent to 36 per cent of all their ventures established by 1987. Hong Kong had the highest and the US and other developed countries had their lowest percentages, Singapore was in the middle. In the following year when overall foreign direct investment inflow into China crashed, Hong Kong investors retrenched and only established 17 per cent of all their ventures in that year, only half of that in the previous year. The year 1987 sees a little recovery with 24 per cent of Hong Kong's venture established in that year. Providing a stark contrast, investors from US and developed countries seemed undaunted as a whole and still established 27 per cent of their ventures and followed by another 26 per cent in 1987. Singapore's venture establishment rate was also slashed in 1986, but not to the same extent as that shown by Hong Kong investors.

All these show one thing: investors from Hong Kong were more sensitive to any policy and environmental changes. This is mainly because of the small size, low technology, and labor intensive investment whose firm specific advantages lay in some special niches provided by policy framework, factor costs, and investment environment. Their advantages may also lie in their established marketing network, flexible management and agility to adopt the market changes. On the contrary, firm specific advantages of developed countries can usually be identified with some intangible assets such as technological expertise or brand names of products. It is the market of host countries that motivate the investors in the first place. As such they are more likely to make a long term commitment and are less swayed by temporary policy and environmental changes.

140

Social and physical distance and location patterns

The third source of deviation of locational patterns among different home countries derive from the difference of their social and geographical distances from different cities. Obviously, the spatial variation of this relationship among the recipient cities must also exist to make the factor relevant to locational patterns.

This host-home distance factor certainly made a difference between the locational patterns of foreign direct investment from Hong Kong, Macau, and Singapore on the one hand, and the location pattern of foreign direct investment from other countries on the other. The close social ties between investors from Hong Kong, Macau, and Singapore and Guangdong and Fujian Provinces made the two provinces their major locational choices.

Conclusion

When we hold the third dimension, the dynamic dimension, of our conceptual framework constant, we can test the multidimensional characteristics of the second dimension, the firm specific characteristics. What was done in this chapter is just that. It has been tested and shown that a country of origin effect on the spatial location of foreign direct investment in China did exist. This effect is shown within two different contexts, the presence of foreign direct investment from different home countries and the spatial distribution of the accumulation of investment in space.

For investors from Hong Kong and Singapore, the social and physical distance between their home and host cities in China was important for both their presence and their final locational decisions. For investors from developed countries, however, while they perceived that city size and special policy as important for their presence, they chose their final locations of production based on the true merits of cities, i.e., large scale of existing manufacturing activity and local market and better infrastructures and/or higher level of consumption.

Notes

1   Foreign direct investment from European countries was mostly made by Germany, Britain, and France. Small amounts of investment from other western and north European countries such as Sweden are also included in this category.

2   Refer to John H. Aldrich and Forrest D. Nelson, *Linear Probability, Logit, and Probit Models*, Sage Publications: Beverly Hills, CA, 1984.

3   This is done by using cluster analysis. Refer to Mark S. Aldenderfer and Roger K. Blashfield, *Cluster Analysis*, Sage Publications: Beverly Hills, CA, 1984. The cosine of vectors of variables, which is really a pattern similarity measure, is used to measure the distance between countries.

Countries are combined into clusters in a way such that the average difference among all cases in a resulting group is as small as possible.

8 Conclusions

On the process of China's opening to the world since 1979

China's opening to the world has been a step-by-step effort since 1979. Foreign direct investment involvement can be divided into four stages along with the policy changes and improvements in the investment environment in China. A slow start and an unimpressive performance marked the first four years of China's opening experience. A short-lived boom started in late 1984 and peaked in 1985. Within a bandwagon atmosphere, foreign direct investment pledged in 1985 doubled that in 1984. Immediately following was a crash that started in early 1986 and was marked by a slashing of the amount of foreign direct investment inflow and a temporary loss of foreign investors' confidence. The years 1987 to 1990 marked the third period of foreign direct investment involvement in China, which could be characterized as a period of quick recovery and a temporary interruption in 1989. This new stage was made possible by a flurry of legislative activity that started in late 1986 and by some serious efforts made by the Chinese central and local governments to align China's investment environment with international standards. Starting from 1991, the involvement of foreign direct investment has entered a full-fledged stage characterized by a huge increase of foreign direct investment inflow each year. The amount of foreign direct investment pledged in 1992 alone reached 58 billion dollars. It is now at a decisive moment for both sides: foreign investors and China.

On the locational framework for foreign direct investment within a subnational context

The location of foreign direct investment within a subnational context should be distinguished clearly from that within a national context. The location of foreign direct investment within the two different contexts belongs to two levels of MNE planning. Choosing which market to enter belongs in the realm of strategic planning of MNEs. Market size, political stability, and the investment environment of different countries are the major locational determinants. After an MNE chooses to enter a specific market (country), the specific location for its production is within the domain of tactical planning. Its main concern in the tactical planning process is the optimization of the operation. Some factors such as political stability may play a critical role in MNEs' strategic planning process, but can have little impact once an MNE has chosen a market. As such, within these two different levels of decision making, both the objectives and settings are different. Moreover, the relationships among the potential hosts for international production are different within the two different locational contexts.

A locational framework for the location of foreign direct investment within a subnational context can be built upon a simple MNE model. This simple MNE model stipulates that an MNE's decision making as an economic entity is based on both its internal factors and environmental factors that are exogenous to the MNE. The framework includes three dimensions: firm specific variables (FSVs), locational specific variables (LSVs), and one dynamic (temporal) dimension. While the first two dimensions are derived from the simple MNE model, the third dimension is critical to understanding foreign direct investment location in time and space. Multinational enterprises respond to environmental factors in the short run and evolve and interact with environment in the long run. The evolutionary changes in both the environment and MNEs plus the interaction between the two dimensions form the dynamic dimension of this framework.

Each dimension is also a multidimensional structure. The dimension of FSVs refers not only to firm specific advantages as in foreign direct investment theories, but also to other relevant firm characteristics. These characteristics can be identified by countries, sectors, the position in a product cycle, and also by firm strategies. All these aspects can affect the objectives and relevant location factors. In other words, firm specific advantages can only be identified with a different set, or certain geographical pattern of LSVs.

The second dimension, LSVs, includes a host of variables that are usually identified by location theory and reflect a host region's social and economic reality and government policy. This dimension should also include environmental aspects (exogenous to a specific MNE) which affect an MNE's locational decision. One such aspect is the behaviour (locational strategy) of other MNEs in the same industry. The oligopolistic reactions of MNEs usually create a 'following the leader' phenomenon whose spatial consequences are concentration of foreign direct investment in space. Other factors such as social and physical distance between home and host countries identified in foreign direct investment literature are also a part of the package of LSVs presented by a host region to a specific MNE. This second dimension also has two properties. First, all the LSVs are related and should be viewed as a system. Second, any configuration of these LSVs exists at just one point in time; a cross-section of a dynamic process of regional transformation.

The dynamic dimension stipulates that the location of foreign direct investment is a dynamic process within which the location of foreign direct investment at a point in time is affected by not only the original environmental factors, but also by changes in the environment induced by the evolutionary forces and by the participation of foreign direct investment of a previous period, and by the existence of foreign direct investment of a previous period. Foreign direct investment induces environmental changes in two ways. First, a new equilibrium of factor markets results from the disturbance induced by the presence of foreign direct investment in a local economy. Second, the industrial structure in the host region changes because of the presence of foreign direct investment. The changes in industrial structure may affect three sets of firm relationships: relationships among indigenous firms, relationships among FIVs, and that between FIVs and indigenous firms. The changes induced by the foreign direct investment of a previous period can work both ways for the foreign direct investment of the next period and have different spatial implications. Market efficiency induced by previous foreign direct investment, especially in a planned economic system, will induce foreign direct investment to accumulate in space. Increased factor costs, marginal profitability and investment opportunities may lead new investors to seek new locations. The experience effect may help reinvestment and new investment accumulate in certain locations where foreign investors are familiar and had successful experiences.

The framework is a comprehensive one, without which a thorough understanding of location of foreign direct investment within a subnational context may not be possible. Many locationally related issues can be guided by and examined within this framework.

On the general locational models of foreign direct investment in China

A series of cross section analyzes on the locational model of foreign direct investment in China was conducted. It is both a test of the validity of the third dimension of the framework and model building for the location of foreign direct investment within the Chinese context: a planned economy with a potential huge market. The dynamic nature of foreign direct investment location is proved by the changes of the models and the detection of foreign direct investment realized in a previous period affecting the inflow of foreign direct investment in following periods.

Overall, the most important locational determinant is the city size factor represented mostly by RETAILVAL, local retail value, and sometimes by urban population. This factor is not directly called a market factor on two accounts. First, a prefecture level city in China cannot be considered as a separate market in a conventional sense. Second, the strong relationship between RETAILVAL and other city size variables such as the manufacturing output and urban population, makes one reluctant to conclude that RETAILVAL is strictly a market factor.

Yet, the market content of this factor increases during the process. This assertion is supported by the joining of such variables as consumption level and market potential of a city with RETAILVAL. The market potential is a reflection of the market of a province and its geographical location with reference to other provinces.

Policy instruments have been used extensively by the Chinese government to attract desired foreign direct investment and affect the distribution in line with government regional economic development policy. While the impact on the quality of foreign direct investment is not tested in this analysis, the impact of policy instruments on the location of foreign direct investment is proven. Foreign direct investment has been channeled to special regional entities such as SEZs, COCs and CORs. However, this impact has been waning since 1991.

One should not equate policy instruments totally with preferential treatments in the foreign direct investment literature. While preferential treatment toward foreign direct investment is an important part of policy instruments, the special policy in China also entails significant autonomous power for local city governments with more relaxed government control. In this sense, the policy design was also intended to create micro environments in line with international standards within a still mainly planned system. As such, the importance of policy instruments means more than investors being attracted to preferential treatments such as tax reduction. The waning effect of policy variables also shows the experience effect. As foreign investors gain more experience, they venture out of their familiar territories created by special policies.

Other factors such as host-home social and physical distances and large urban centers are relevant. Factors such as better infrastructures, the experience effect, dynamic economic environment and growth are also strongly implied by the models.

The implication of the dynamic change of location models is the spatial diffusion of foreign direct investment in China. These changes include market factors becoming more important and the disappearing of the policy variables that reflect only part of the coastal area.

Latent variable model versus factual variable model

Two sets of location models are built in this analysis. One set is the latent variable models and the other set is the factual variable models, with the former built upon calculated indices reflecting the basic dimensions of possible locational choices. The latter is a set of models built directly upon actual urban statistics. They are also built on different assumptions. The latent variable models assume that foreign investors are responsive to the basic characteristics of cities, while the factual variable models assume that foreign investors are attracted to specific attributes of cities.

Both sets of models are efficient ways to reveal the location patterns. With the former, the basic dimensions underlying the location of foreign direct investment can be easily discovered. The factual variable model can be used to test the impact of specific variables. Also, the latent variables are more appropriate to the foreign direct investment location patterns when the involvement of foreign direct investment in a country enters a mature stage.

On the locational characteristics of the presence of foreign direct investment

The book also takes the initiative to study the locational characteristics of the presence of foreign direct investment. It is based on the assumption that the location decision of MNEs, or any economic entity for that matter, involves two steps. First, some locations are considered unsuitable and excluded from further consideration based on certain criteria. For the location of international production within a national context, political instability and social unrest in some countries may disqualify these countries as a locational choice in the first place. Second, the final location choices are made by assessing the relative merits of those possible locations left after the first step.

As such, at a point in time, the difference between a host region/country with no foreign direct investment and those with varying amounts of foreign direct investment represents a categorical change, rather than a change of volume. A discriminant analysis between two groups of cities in China found that the criteria that differentiate the two groups are a combination of location, policy, and other urban characteristics such as size, the infrastructure and, market potential; and that these criteria change over time. While the distance from the coast has always been important, the most important urban characteristics measured at an interval scale change from a size factor to an infrastructure factor to a market factor measured in market potential.

Compared with the factors that affect the distribution of foreign direct investment, one can find that the factors determining who gets it or not and factors determining who get more or less are not identical.

On the country of origin effect

When the dynamic change of the general location pattern of foreign direct investment is discussed, the focus is the dynamic change of the model made possible by assuming the homogeneity of foreign direct investment, i.e., the effect of LSVs on every dollar in any location is the same. In other words, diversity of the first dimension is compromised. In Chapter Seven the reverse exercise is conducted by controlling the dynamic (temporal) dimension to examine the impact of FSVs on the location models of foreign direct investment. Only one aspect of this dimension is examined, though, that is the effect of country of origin.

Distinct location behaviour has been found among the major investors (before 1988), namely, Hong Kong, the US, European countries, Japan, and Singapore. Major differences were found between two groups of countries: Hong Kong and Singapore as NICs, and the US, Japan, and European countries as developed countries. For NICs, the host-home distance factor played a dominant role in both its presence and accumulation of investment in space. For investors from developed countries, city size and the policy status of a city did affect a city's odds of becoming a foreign direct investment recipient city. As to the spatial distribution of their investment, the most important determinant is the size of a city; particularly if it is a national and large regional urban center. Urban infrastructures and levels of consumption also made differences in their location patterns.

On the policy implications of this research

This research has two policy implications. One is on the special policy as a whole. Its effectiveness as an instrument to achieve the locational aspects of national development policy is proven. Overall, foreign direct investment has been channeled to coastal regions with special policies of different levels, e.g., SEZ policy, COC policy, and COR policy. Yet, it may be in China's national interest to review its special policy toward foreign direct investment and end some of its preferential treatment in coastal regions. This suggestion is based on three conclusions of this analysis.

First, the impact of special policy on the spatial distribution of foreign direct investment started to decrease in 1991. This shows that foreign investment in China has already entered a more mature stage during which the built-up attributes such as city size and market potential act as the main locational determinants.

Second, up to 1991, the advantages of cities with special policies, especially SEZs and COCs, over other cities had increased tremendously. These advantages are beyond the special policy these cities retain. As such, the continuation of special policy toward these coastal regions may greatly increase regional disparity.

Third, policy measures had more impact on inducing investment from NICs. Investment from these counties is usually low technology and labor intensive. On the other hand, investment from developed countries has a much greater portion of technology intensive investment and its location will not be affected much by special policy. It is China's potential market and the true merit of a location, for example, a well-developed infrastructure, that makes the difference.

The discontinuation of some special policy in coastal areas may discourage the inflow of labor intensive and low technology foreign direct investment, but it will not affect the interest of market seeking investors with distinct ownership advantages. As such, it will not affect the overall objectives of inducing foreign direct investment. Given the tremendous impact of foreign direct investment on local economic development, the Chinese government may need to consider introducing special policies in less developed areas or areas with disadvantaged locations.

Suggestions for future research

The locational framework takes the analysis of this book one step beyond the conventional treatment of the location of foreign direct investment in that the location of foreign direct investment is treated as a dynamic process. However, there is more to be done to improve the framework and to exemplify the flexibility and comprehensive nature of the framework. This mainly concerns the second dimension.

First, the LSVs should always be treated as a system. As mentioned in both Chapter Four and this concluding chapter, the LSVs should be treated as a system not only in that one variable change may induce changes in others (as in a social and economic system), but also in that the assessment of the attractiveness of a host region should be done in total not just based on one or several variables. In other words, one aspect of host regions should be assessed with reference to other aspects of the region. One example for this reasoning is that higher labor cost should be assessed in consideration of labor productivity. In this respect, the latent variable models are appropriate and its implications need to be further explored.

The second dimension as a dynamic system in inducing foreign direct investment needs to be addressed. This requires the pattern of LSVs to be treated as a point in a dynamic process. Regional economies evolve through stages of distinct social and economic structures. A study of the functional relationships between the structure of foreign direct investment against the structure of regional economic transformation will bring our understanding of the impact of location of foreign direct investment to a new level.

A Regression analysis of pledged FDI on latent urban variables

Table A.1

Regression of foreign direct investment pledged in 1985 on 1984 latent urban variables

	Amount of foreign direct investment pledged in 1985
Dependent variable	
r^2	0.47
Degrees of freedom	66
Constant, standard error, t, significance	-7.15, 1.31, -5.44, 0.00
F value, significance	29.13, 0.00
K-S statistic, significance	0.07, >0.20

Variables	Cumulative r squared	Coefficient and standard error	Beta	t value and significance
Level of development	0.31	8.83, 1.34	0.59	6.56, 0.00
Size of city	0.47	5.16, 1.17	0.40	4.42, 0.00

Table A.2

Regression of foreign direct investment pledged in 1987 on 1986 latent urban variables

Dependent variable	Amount of foreign direct investment pledged in 1987
r^2	0.48
Degrees of freedom	58
Constant, standard error, t, significance	-5.64, 1.14, -4.95, 0.00
F value, significance	29.92, 0.00
K-S statistic, significance	0.08, >0.20

Variables	Cumulative r squared	Coefficient and standard error	Beta	t value and significance
Level of development	0.33	7.09, 1.11	0.59	6.36, 0.00
Size of city	0.43	4.68, 1.13	0.39	4.15, 0.00
Variables considered but not in final equation				
Productivity			0.06	0.62, 0.54
Level of urbanization			3.91E-05	0.00, 0.99

153

Table A.3

Regression of foreign direct investment pledged in 1988 on 1986 latent urban variables

	Amount of foreign direct investment pledged in 1988
Dependent variable	
r^2	0.57
Degrees of freedom	68
Constant, standard error, t, significance	-7.42, 1.11, -6.69, 0.00
F value, significance	30.28, 0.00
K-S statistic, significance	0.09, >0.20

Variables	Cumulative r squared	Coefficient and standard error	Beta	t value and significance
Level of development	0.21	5.43, 0.88	0.49	6.14, 0.00
Size of city	0.41	5.28, 0.88	0.47	5.99, 0.00
Productivity	0.57	4.30, 0.87	0.39	4.96, 0.00
Variable considered but not in final equation				
Level of urbanization		-	0.02	0.23, 0.82

Table A.4
Regression of foreign direct investment pledged in 1989 on 1986 latent urban variables

Dependent variable	Amount of foreign direct investment pledged in 1989
r^2	0.60
Degrees of freedom	67
Constant, standard error, t, significance	-7.97, 1.40, -5.71, 0.00
F value, significance	25.43, 0.00
K-S statistic, significance	0.08, >0.20

Variables	Cumulative r squared	Coefficient and standard error	Beta	t value and significance
Level of development	0.30	7.36, 1.01	0.56	7.22, 0.00
Size of city	0.51	6.29, 1.01	0.48	6.22, 0.00
Productivity	0.57	3.34, 1.11	0.23	3.00, 0.00
Level of urbanization	0.60	-1.79, 0.77	-0.18	-2.33, 0.02

Table A.5
Regression of foreign direct investment pledged in 1990 on 1986 latent urban variables

	Amount of foreign direct investment pledged in 1990
Dependent variable	
r^2	0.69
Degrees of freedom	73
Constant, standard error, t, significance	-7.19, 1.05, -6.86, 0.00
F value, significance	40.63, 0.00
K-S statistic, significance	0.07, >0.20

Variables	Cumulative r squared	Coefficient and standard error	Beta	t value and significance
Level of development	0.35	7.38, 0.79	0.61	9.33, 0.00
Size of city	0.57	5.85, 0.79	0.48	7.37, 0.00
Productivity	0.64	3.12, 0.76	0.27	4.10, 0.00
Level of urbanization	0.69	-2.05, 0.59	-0.23	-3.47, 0.00

Table A.6

Regression of foreign direct investment pledged in 1991 on 1986 latent urban variables

Dependent variable	Amount of foreign direct investment pledged in 1991
r^2	0.67
Degrees of freedom	75
Constant, standard error, t, significance	-5.17, 0.98, -5.30, 0.00
F value, significance	37.84, 0.00
K-S statistic, significance	0.07, >0.20

Variables	Cumulative r squared	Coefficient and standard error	Beta	t value and significance
Level of development	0.37	6.84, 0.76	0.60	8.91, 0.00
Size of city	0.57	5.26, 0.74	0.47	7.06, 0.00
Level of urbanization	0.63	-2.19, 0.58	-0.25	-3.81, 0.00
Productivity	0.67	2.04, 0.72	0.19	2.85, 0.01

Table A.7

Regression of foreign direct investment pledged in 1993 on 1991 latent urban variables

Dependent variable	Amount of foreign direct investment pledged in 1993
r^2	0.60
Degrees of freedom	79
Constant, standard error, t, significance	-3.71, 1.03, -3.59, 0.00
F value, significance	40.16, 0.00
K-S statistic, significance	0.08, >0.20

Variables	Cumulative r squared	Coefficient and standard error	Beta	t value and significance
Size of city	0.34	6.95	0.86	8.09, 0.00
Level of development	0.56	6.16, 0.98	0.45	6.31, 0.00
Level of urbanization	0.60	-1.96, 0.68	-0.20	-2.87, 0.00

158

B Regression analysis of FDI on factual urban variables

160

Table B.1

Regression of foreign direct investment pledged in 1985 on 1984 locational variables

Dependent variable	Amount of foreign direct investment pledged in 1985
r^2	0.65
Degrees of freedom	61
Constant, standard error, t, significance	2.94, 0.21, 13.87, 0.00
F value, significance	16.77, 0.00
K-S statistic, significance	0.06, >0.20

Variables	Cumulative r squared	Coefficient and standard error	Beta	Tolerance level	t value and significance
RETAILVAL	0.26	1.92E-06, 3.94E-07	0.40	0.83	4.88, 0.00
SEZPOLICY	0.43	1.33, 0.41	0.27	0.77	3.20, 0.00
DSADJACEN	0.49	1.25, 0.31	0.35	0.72	4.01, 0.00
MP	0.54	-2.08E-05, 4.70E-06	-0.38	0.77	-4.44, 0.00
DCINLAND	0.60	-0.41, 0.18	-0.19	0.80	-2.30, 0.02
RCENTER	0.63	0.65, 0.24	0.22	0.81	2.63, 0.01
COCPOLICY	0.66	0.51, 0.22	0.19	0.82	2.30, 0.03

Table B.2
Regression of foreign direct investment pledged in 1986 on 1984 locational variables

Dependent variable	Amount of foreign direct investment pledged in 1986
r^2	0.59
Degrees of freedom	64
Constant, standard error, t, significance	2.09, 0.12, 17.11, 0.00
F value, significance	18.04, 0.00
K-S statistic, significance	0.10, >0.18

Variables	Cumulative r squared	Coefficient and standard error	Beta	Tolerance level	t value and significance
RETAILVAL	0.34	2.44E-06, 3.86E-07	0.53	0.91	6.31, 0.00
SEZPOLICY	0.045	1.08, 0.42	0.23	0.78	2.55, 0.01
RCENTER	0.49	0.66, 0.24	0.24	0.90	2.76, 0.01
DCCOAST	0.54	-0.51, 0.16	-0.27	0.95	-3.21, 0.00
DSADJACEN	0.59	0.81, 0.31	0.24	0.77	2.62, 0.01

161

Table B.3
Regression of foreign direct investment pledged in 1987 on 1986 locational variables

Dependent variable	Amount of foreign direct investment pledged in 1987
r^2	0.45
Degrees of freedom	59
Constant, standard error, t, significance	2.38, 0.13, 18.02, 0.00
F value, significance	15.91, 0.00
K-S statistic, significance	0.07, >0.20

Variables	Cumulative r squared	Coefficient and standard error	Beta	Tolerance level	t value and significance
FDISUM (1978-1986)	0.28	0.67E-05, 6.16E-06	0.43	0.94	4.33, 0.00
URBANPOP	0.39	2.4E-05, 6.53E-06	0.32	0.96	3.27, 0.00
DCINLAND	0.45	-0.49, 0.20	-0.24	0.97	-2.51, 0.01

Table B.4

Regression of foreign direct investment pledged in 1988 on 1986 locational variables

Dependent variable	Amount of foreign direct investment pledged in 1988			
r^2	0.63			
Degrees of freedom	66			
Constant, standard error, t, significance	2.31, 0.11, 20.98, 0.00			
F value, significance	18.89, 0.00			
K-S statistic, significance	0.04, >0.20			

Variables	Cumulative r squared	Coefficient and standard error	Beta	Tolerance level	t value and significance
URBANPOP	0.23	2.70E-05, 4.94E-06	0.44	0.87	5.47, 0.00
SEZPOLICY	0.44	1.39, 0.36	0.35	0.66	3.85, 0.00
COCPOLICY	0.52	0.58, 0.18	0.26	0.89	3.24, 0.00
RCENTER	0.57	0.58, 0.16	0.28	0.92	3.63, 0.00
KLRATIO	0.60	0.0014, 5.61E-04	0.17	0.96	2.42, 0.02
DSADJACEN	0.63	0.71, 0.31	0.21	0.66	2.26, 0.03

163

Table B.5
Regression of foreign direct investment pledged in 1989 on 1986 locational variables

Dependent variable		Amount of foreign direct investment pledged in 1989				
r^2		0.59				
Degrees of freedom		67				
Constant, standard error, t, significance		2.07, 0.10, 20.37, 0.00				
F value, significance		23.75, 0.00				
K-S statistic, significance		0.06, >0.20				

Variables	Cumulative r squared	Coefficient and standard error	Beta	Tolerance level	t value and significance
DCPORT	0.29	0.80, 0.19	0.36	0.89	4.26, 0.00
RETAILVAL	0.42	1.13E-06, 2.56E-07	0.37	0.88	4.39, 0.00
SEZPOLICY	0.54	1.77, 038	0.38	0.92	4.70, 0.00
RCENTER	0.59	0.51, 0.19	0.21	0.93	2.62, 0.00

Table B.6
Regression of foreign direct investment pledged in 1990 on 1986 locational variables

Dependent variable	Amount of foreign direct investment pledged in 1990	
r^2	0.70	
Degrees of freedom	70	
Constant, standard error, t, significance	2.92, 0.29, 10.12, 0.00	
F value, significance	22.98, 0.00	
K-S statistic, significance	0.05, >0.20	

Variables	Cumulative r squared	Coefficient and standard error	Beta	Tolerance level	t value and significance
RETAILVAL	0.28	1.08E-06, 2.05E-07	0.38	0.83	5.27, 0.00
SEZPOLICY	0.50	0.23, 0.29	0.51	0.93	7.61, 0.00
COCPOLICY	0.58	0.82, 0.19	0.33	0.74	4.35, 0.00
CORPOLICY	0.64	0.43, 0.15	0.22	0.69	2.82, 0.00
RCENTER	0.66	0.40, 0.16	0.18	0.80	2.50, 0.00
MP	0.68	7.86-E06, 3.48E-06	-0.17	0.78	-2.26, 0.03
VALADD%	0.70	-0.015, 0.007	-0.14	0.85	-2.02, 0.05

Table B.7
Regression of foreign direct investment pledged in 1991 on 1986 locational variables

Dependent variable	Amount of foreign direct investment pledged in 1991
r^2	0.68
Degrees of freedom	74
Constant, standard error, t, significance	2.56, 0.07, 34.23, 0.00
F value, significance	30.89, 0.00
K-S statistic, significance	0.08, >0.20

Variables	Cumulative r squared	Coefficient and standard error	Beta	Tolerance level	t value and significance
RETAILVAL	0.27	9.56E-07, 1.94E-07	0.36	0.83	4.97, 0.00
SEZPOLICY	0.48	2.10, 0.27	0.51	0.98	7.69, 0.00
COCPOLICY	0.56	0.87, 0.17	0.37	0.81	5.02, 0.00
CORPOLICY	0.65	0.43, 0.13	0.24	0.82	3.23, 0.00
RCENTER	0.68	0.40, 0.15	0.19	0.82	2.61, 0.01

Table B.8

Regression of foreign direct investment pledged in 1992 on 1991 locational variables

Dependent variable	Amount of foreign direct investment pledged in 1992
r^2	0.58
Degrees of freedom	78
Constant, standard error, t, significance	1.96, 0.33, 5.96, 0.00
F value, significance	21.28, 0.00
K-S statistic, significance	0.06, >0.20

Variables	Cumulative r squared	Coefficient and standard error	Beta	Tolerance level	t value and significance
RETAILVAL	0.28	4.12E-07, 1.18E-07	0.29	0.81	3.49, 0.00
RATERETL (1986-1991)	0.43	0.08, 0.02	0.29	0.89	3.67, 0.00
RCENTER	0.50	0.67, 0.19	0.27	0.91	3.47, 0.00
DCPORT	0.55	0.62, 0.18	0.27	0.86	3.45, 0.00
TAXWELL	0.58	2.69, 1.28	0.16	0.90	2.11, 0.04

Table B.9

Regression of foreign direct investment pledged in 1992 to 1993 on 1991 locational variables

Dependent variable	Amount of foreign direct investment pledged in 1992 and 1993
r^2	0.63
Degrees of freedom	76
Constant, standard error, t, significance	2.25, 0.31, 7.17, 0.00
F value, significance	21.26, 0.00
K-S statistic, significance	0.08, >0.20

Variables	Cumulative r squared	Coefficient and standard error	Beta	Tolerance level	t value and significance
RETAILVAL	0.33	4.23E-07, 1.10E-07	0.30	0.77	3.84, 0.00
RATERETL	0.46	0.09, 0.02	0.31	0.90	4.28, 0.00
RCENTER	0.53	0.48, 0.18	0.20	0.82	2.61, 0.01
COCPOLICY	0.57	0.74, 0.20	0.29	0.81	3.70, 0.00
CORPOLICY	0.61	0.43, 0.15	0.21	0.85	2.83, 0.00
TAXWELL	0.63	2.32, 1.16	0.15	0.92	2.01, 0.05

C Implication of policy dummy variables

Table C.1
Implication of policy variables for urban characteristics at 1984

Locational variables	National average (100)	Cities with no policy (81)	Cities with COR policy (5)	Cities with COC policy (11)	Cities with SEZ policy (3)	ANOVA (0,3) f, significance	ANOVA (0,2) f, significance
URBANPOP	10454	9961	6407	17982	2894	2.45, 0.06	2.89, 0.06
RETAILVAL	162199	139612	176561	333033	121702	3.97, 0.01*	5.76, 0.00*
OUTPUT	452153	350410	525427	-	126287	4.40, 0.01*	6.21, 0.00*
MP84	37106	34916	54282	44133	41850	2.69, 0.05*	3.96, 0.02*
FDISUM84	1345	571	622	971	24812	27.27, 0.00*	0.07, 0.93
GAP	2.89	2.81	3.56	3.42	1.84	1.07, 0.36	1.01, 0.37
AVERETAIL	5.09	4.36	5.01	4.87	25.51	33.48, 0.00*	0.69, 0.51
AVEWORKOUT	46.82	46.60	49.66	46.59	490.02	0.00, 1.00	0.00, 1.00
WAGE	11.34	11.54	10.19	9.65	13.85	0.13, 0.94	0.12, 0.88

Table C.1
Implication of policy variables for urban characteristics at 1984
(continued)

Locational variables	National average (100)	Cities with no policy (81)	Cities with COR policy (5)	Cities with COC policy (11)	Cities with SEZ policy (3)	ANOVA (0,3) f, significance	ANOVA (0,2) f, significance
AVEPIPE	0.02	0.02	0.02	0.02	0.06	7.32, 0.00*	2.35, 0.10
TAXWELL	0.17	0.17	0.15	0.18	0.15	0.37, 0.77	0.30, 0.74
URBANPOP%	36	38	21	26	44	2.03, 0.11	2.78, 0.07
OUTPUT%	74	75	67	68	81	1.45, 0.23	1.74, 0.18
VALADD%	32	33	26	30	21	1.80, 0.15	1.16, 0.32
RESIDOUT%	1.54	0.67	2.24	2.64	19.71	15.0, 0.00*	4.09, 0.02*

* test statistic is significant at five per cent error level

Table C.2
Implication of policy variables for urban characteristics at 1986

Locational variables	National average (100)	Cities with no policy (81)	Cities with COR policy (5)	Cities with COC policy (11)	Cities with SEZ policy (3)	ANOVA (0,3) f, significance	ANOVA (0,2) f, significance
URBANPOP	10808	9721	10224	20156	3270	2.78, 0.05*	3.43, 0.04*
RETAILVAL	229827	169560	268376	503728	168871	4.61, 0.01*	6.70, 0.00*
OUTPUT	654368	400168	851654	-	228757	5.63, 0.00*	7.99, 0.00*
MP84	37516	32002	50339	42179	41850	6.45, 0.00*	9.72, 0.00*
FDISUM84	3055	842	398	5706	49472	31.58, 0.00*	4.60, 0.01*
GAP	2.51	2.44	2.78	2.68	1.68	0.67, 0.57	0.45, 0.64
AVERETAIL	6.99	5.83	6.65	7.17	29.91	29.28, 0.00*	1.63, 0.20
AVEWORKOUT	61.94	54.98	67.53	68.74	131.39	2.73, 0.05	0.82, 0.45
WAGE	15.46	14.95	14.01	15.63	33.34	3.66, 0.02*	0.13, 0.88
AVEPIPE	0.02	0.02	0.03	0.03	0.07	18.52, 0.00*	10.72, 0.00*

172

Table C.2
Implication of policy variables for urban characteristics at 1986
(continued)

Locational variables	National average (100)	Cities with no policy (81)	Cities with COR policy (5)	Cities with COC policy (11)	Cities with SEZ policy (3)	ANOVA (0,3) f, significance	ANOVA (0,2) f, significance
KLRATIO	118	126	96	96	175	0.88, 0.46	0.78, 0.46
TAXWELL	0.16	0.16	0.15	0.15	0.12	0.37, 0.78	0.17, 0.84
URBANPOP%	37	41	27	29	47	3.13, 0.03*	4.20, 0.02*
OUTPUT%	81	82	77	80	88	0.87, 0.46	0.98, 0.38
VALADD%	30	32	27	25	24	3.64, 0.02*	4.86, 0.01*
RESIDOUT%	12	9	14	18	37	6.21, 0.00*	3.03, 0.05*
RATEOUT	21.63	18.42	26.9	26.68	30.39	3.66, 0.02*	4.65, 0.01*
RATERETL	19.53	18.47	21.6	21.4	19.43	1.70, 0.17	2.82, 0.07
RATEPIPE	23.6	24.98	11.8	27.15	61.22	0.57, 0.63	0.35, 0.71

* test statistic is significant at five per cent error level

173

Table C.3
Implication of policy variables for urban characteristics at 1991

Locational variables	National average (100)	Cities with no policy (81)	Cities with COR policy (5)	Cities with COC policy (11)	Cities with SEZ policy (3)	ANOVA (0,3) f, significance	ANOVA (0,2) f, significance
URBANPOP	11984	10646	11123	23251	4415	3.12, 0.03*	4.04, 0.02*
RETAILVAL	469935	344245	528237	-	500934	4.35, 0.01*	6.40, 0.00*
OUTPUT	-	-	-	-	-	5.39, 0.00*	7.94, 0.00*
MP91	102589	83898	141150	121897	136659	9.43, 0.00*	13.75, 0.00*
FDISUM91	14165	4629	3961	48058	140644	16.84, 0.00*	8.05, 0.00*
GAP	2.29	2.34	2.22	2.38	1.53	0.48, 0.70	0.08, 0.92
AVERETAIL	13.38	10.69	12.18	14.09	68	43.13, 0.00*	2.05, 0.13
AVEWOKOUT	70.42	78.14	55.76	49.73	90.71	0.13, 0.94	0.17, 0.85
WAGE	24.9	23.61	24.9	26.54	43.23	36.94, 0.00*	4.50, 0.01*
AVEPIPE	0.04	0.02	0.03	0.11	0.07	3.43, 0.02*	4.78, 0.01*

Table C.3
Implication of policy variables for urban characteristics at 1991
(continued)

Locational variables	National average (100)	Cities with no policy (81)	Cities with COR policy (5)	Cities with COC policy (11)	Cities with SEZ policy (3)	ANOVA (0,3) f, significance	ANOVA (0,2) f, significance
KLRATIO	142	168	95	81	156	0.42, 0.24	0.62, 0.54
TAXWELL	0.09	0.09	0.09	0.09	0.09	0.12, 0.95	0.16, 0.85
URBANPOP%	38	41	27	31	55	3.00, 0.04*	3.29, 0.04*
OUTPUT%	83	82	84	79	92	1.34, 0.27	0.57, 0.57
VALADD%	26	27	24	25	25	1.91, 0.14	2.71, 0.07
RESIDOUT%	14	12	21	20	5	9.64, 0.00*	11.82, 0.00*
RATEOUT	22	21	22	23	49	26.07, 0.00*	1.00, 0.37
RATERETL	15	14	14	16	24	16.76, 0.00*	2.53, 0.08
RATEPIPE	11	12	6	14	10	1.09, 0.36	1.58, 0.21

* test statistic is significant at five per cent error level

D List of abbreviations

ATVs	Advanced technology ventures
CJVs	Cooperative joint ventures
COCs	Coastal open cities
CORs	Coastal open regions
EJVs	Equity joint ventures
EOVs	Export-oriented ventures
ETDZs	Economic and technology development zones
FDI	Foreign direct investment
FIVs	Foreign invested ventures
FSVs	Firm specific variables
HTDZs	High and new technology industry development zones
ICCT	Industrial and commercial consolidation tax
JEPs	Joint exploration projects
LDCs	Less developed countries
LSVs	Location specific variables
MNEs	Multinational enterprises
MOFERT	the Ministry of Foreign Economic Relations and Trade

NICs	Newly industrialized countries
RMB	Reminbi, the Chinese currency
SEZs	Special economic zone
WFVs	Wholly foreign owned ventures
the Almanac	the Almanac of China's Foreign Economic Relations and Trade, which is published by the MOFERT yearly.

E Definition of variables

AMOUTPUT   gross output value of agriculture and manufacturing industry, in RMB¥(0000s)

AVEAMOUT   gross output value of agriculture and manufacturing industry per capita, in RMB¥(0000s)

AVEFIRMOUT gross manufacturing output per firm (state owned and collectively owned enterprise), in RMB¥(0000s)

AVELECTRI   electricity consumption per capita per year, in KWH

AVENETOUT   net manufacturing output (value added) per capita, in RMB¥ (0000s)

AVEPHONE   number of phones per capita in urban area, in number

AVEPIPE   the length of urban underground sewage pipes per capita, in kilometers

AVERETAIL   total retail value per capita, in RMB¥(0000s)

AVESAVE   saving per capita in urban area, in RMB¥(0000s)

AVEWOKOUT   productivity of labour measured in net manufacturing output per worker (state-owned and collectively owned enterprises), RMB¥(0000s)

COCPOLICY   dummy variable designated for COCs

CORPOLICY   dummy variable designated for CORs

DCCOAST   dummy variable designated for cities other than coastal port city but are still situated in a coastal provinces

DCINLAND   dummy variable designated for cities in inland provinces which include all the provinces other than coastal provinces and Neimeng, Xinjiang, Qinghai, Xizang, Yunnan, and Guizhou Provinces

DCPORT   dummy variable designated for coastal port cities

DSADJACEN   dummy variable designated for cities in Guangdong Province where distance from source country is in "adjacent" category, which means a city is both socially and geographically adjacent to at least one of the source countries

DSCLOSE   dummy variable designated for cities in Fujian Province where the distance from source country is in a category which a city is both socially and geographically very close, although to a lesser degree than cities adjacent, to at least one home country.

ELECTRIC   total amount of electricity used each year by both industries and residents, in KWH

EMPLOYEE   the total number of employees in state and collectively owned enterprises and institutions, in (0,000)s

GAP   inequity of development between the urban area and the periphery of a city, which is expressed in terms of the ratio of the gross manufacturing output per capita in urban area to the average of the city

KLRATIO   capital labour ratio measured in net fixed capital per worker, in RMB¥(0000s)

MP84, MP86, market potential of cities using 1984, 1986, 1991 urban statistics
MP91

MP   market potential of a city, refer to Note 1 in Chapter Five

180

NCENTER	dummy variable designated for national urban and economic centres such as Beijing and Shanghai.
NETFIXK	total net fixed capital, in RMB¥(0000s)
NETFIXK%	percentage of net fixed capital within total fixed capital
NONAPOP%	percentage of a city's population registered as non-agricultural residents
NUMPHONE	number of telephone in urban area
OUTPUT	total gross output value of manufacturing industry, in RMB¥(0000s)
OUTPUT%	percentage of total gross output value of manufacturing industry within the total gross output value of agriculture and manufacturing industry, in RMB¥(0000s)
RATEOUT	growth rate of gross output value in manufacturing industry, in per cent
RATEPIPE	growth rate of the length of urban underground sewage pipes, in per cent
RATERETL	growth rate of the total retail value, in per cent
RCNETER	dummy variable designated for regional major industrial and urban centres (based on urban population size and size of manufacturing industry)
RESIDOUT%	percentage of gross manufacturing output value produced by enterprises other than state and collectively owned enterprises
RETAILVAL	total retail value of a city, RMB¥(0000s)
SCIENCPOP	number of employees having middle or higher level of professional certificates
SEZPOLICY	dummy variable designated for SEZs
SOEOUT%	gross manufacturing output value produced by state owned enterprise, in per cent

181

TAXWELL   tax and profit ability of a local economy measured by the propor-
               tion of gross manufacturing output value submitted as tax and profit
               to the state, in per cent

URBANPOP   the number of people living in a urban proper which is officially
               designated as urban

URBANPOP%   percentage of people living in urban area within the total population
               of a city

VALADD%   percentage of value added in manufacturing industry within the
               total gross output value

VALUEADD   value added (net output value) of manufacturing industry, in
               RMB¥(0000s)

WAGE   labour cost measured by annual wage per worker in state and
               collectively owned enterprises in urban area, in RMB¥(0000s)

References

Agarwal, J. P. (1980), 'Determinants of foreign investment: a survey', *Weltwirtschaftliche Archiv.*, 116(4), pp.739-73.

Aharoni, Y. (1966), 'The foreign investment decision process', Harvard University Press: Boston.

Ajami, R. A. and D. A. Ricks (1981), 'Motives for the American firms investing in the United States', *Journal of International Business Studies*, 12, pp.25-46.

Alexanderson, G. (1956), 'The industrial structure of American cities', University of Nebraska Press: Lincoln, Nebraska.

Ansoff, H. I. (1965), *Corporate strategy: an analytical approach to business policy for growth and expansion*, McGraw-Hill: New York.

Arpan, J. and D. A. Ricks (1974), 'Foreign direct investment in the US and some attendant research problems', *Journal of International Business Studies*, 5, pp.1-8.

Bagchi-Sen S. and J. O. Wheeler (1989), 'A spatial and temporal model of foreign direct investment in the United States', *Economic Geography*, 65(2), pp.113-29.

Balasubramanyam, V. H. (1986), 'Incentives and disincentives for foreign direct investment in less developed countries', in B. Blassa (ed.) *Economic Incentives: Proceedings of A Conference Held by the Economic Association at Kiel, West Germany*, St. Martin's: Press New York, pp.416-25.

Baldwin, R. E. (1979), 'Determinants of trade and foreign investment: further evidence', *The Review of Economics and Statistics*, 61(1), pp.40-48.

Ballance, R. H., J. Ansori and H. W. Singer (1982), *The International Economy and Industrial Development: the Impact of Trade and Investment on the Third World*, Wheatsheaf: Brighton.

Beamish, P. W. (1987), 'Joint ventures in LDCs: partner selection and performance', MIR, 27(1), pp.23-37.

Beamish, P. W. and J. C. Banks (1987), 'Equity joint ventures and the theory of the multinational enterprise', *Journal of International Business Studies*, 17, pp.1-16.

Beamish, P. W. and H. Y. Wang (1989), 'Investing in China via joint ventures', *Management International Review*, 29, pp.57-64.

183

Benito, G. R. and G. Gripsrud (1995), 'The internalization process approach to the location of foreign direct investment: an empirical analysis', in M. B. Green and R. McNaughton (eds.), *The Location of Foreign Direct Investment*, Avebury: Brookfield, pp.43-58.

Birkinshaw, J. M. and A. J. Morrison (1995), 'Configurations of strategy and structure in subsidiaries of multinational corporations', *Journal of International Business Studies*, 26(4), pp.729-53.

Blackbourn, A. (1974), 'The spatial behaviour of American firms in Western Europe', in F. E. Hamilton (ed.) *Spatial Perspectives on Industrial Organization and Decision-making*, John Wiley and Sons: London, pp.245-64.

Blackbourn, A. (1972), 'The location of foreign-owned manufacturing plants in the Republic of Ireland', *Tijdschrift Voor Econ. en Soc. Geografie*, 73, pp.438-43.

Bochert, J. R. (1978), 'Major control points in American economic geography', *Annals of the Association of American Geographers*, 62, pp.214-32.

Bower, J. L. and Y. Doz (1979), 'Strategy formulation: a social and political process', in D. Schendel and C. Hofer (eds.) *Strategic Management*, Little and Brown: Boston, pp.152-66.

Brewer, T. L. (1993), 'Government policies, market imperfections, and foreign direct investment', *Journal of International Business Studies*, 24, pp.101-20.

Britton, J. H. (1974), 'Environmental adaption of industrial plants: service linkages, locational environment and organization', in F. E. Hamilton (ed.) *Spatial Perspectives on Industrial Organization and Decision-making*, John Wiley and Sons:London, pp.363-92.

Brooks, G. R. (1995), 'Defining market boundaries', *Strategic Management Journal*, 16, pp.535-49.

Buckley, P. J. (1988), 'The limits of explanation: testing the internalization theory of the multinational enterprise', *Journal of International Business Studies*, 19(2), pp.181-98.

Buckley, P. J. (1983), 'Macroeconomic versus international business approach to direct foreign investment: a comment on Professor Kojima's interpretation', *Hitotshubashi Journal of Economics*, 24(1), pp.95-100.

Buckley, P. and M. Casson (1991), *The Future of the Multinational Enterprise*, 2nd edition, Macmillian: London.

Buckley, P. and M. Casson (1988), 'The theory of cooperation in international business', in F. Contractor and P. Lorange, (eds.) *Cooperative Strategies in International Business*, Lexington Books: Lexington, Mass, pp.31-53.

Burns, L. S. (1977), 'The location of the headquarters of industrial companies: a comment', *Urban Studies*, 14, pp.211-14.

Calvet, A. L. (1981), 'A synthesis of foreign direct investment theories and theories of multinational firm', *Journal of International Business Studies*, 12(1), pp.43-59.

Caves, R.E. (1971), 'International corporations: the industrial economics of foreign investment', *Economica*, 38, pp.1-27.

Caves, R.E. (1974a), 'Multinational firms, competition, and productivity in host-country markets', *Economica*, 41, pp.176-93.

Caves, R.E. (1974b), 'Causes of direct investment: foreign firms' shares in Canadian and United Kingdom manufacturing industries', *The Review of Economics and Statistics*, 56, pp.279-93.

Caves, R.E. (1974c), 'Industrial organization', in J. H. Dunning (ed.), *Economic Analysis and the Multinational Enterprise*, George Allen and Unwin: London, pp.115-46.

Chandler, A. D. (1962), *Strategy and Structure: Chapters in the History of the Industrial Enterprise*, MIT Press: Cambridge, Mass.

Chen, T. J. (1992), 'Determinants of Taiwan's direct foreign investment', *Journal of Development Economics*, 39, pp.397-407.

Chen, E. (1983), 'The multinationals from Hong Kong', in Lall, S. et al. *The New Multinationals: the Spread of Third World Enterprises*, John Wiley: Chichester, pp.88-127.

Chenery, H. B. (1988), 'Industrialization and growth: alternative views of East Asia', in H. Hughes (ed.), *Achieving Industrialization in East Asia*, Cambridge University Press: Cambridge, pp.39-63.

Chenery, H. B., S. Robinson and M. Syrquin (1986), *Industrialization and Growth: A Comparative Study*, Oxford University Press, Cambridge.

Chenery, H. B. (1979), *Structure Change and Development Policy*, Oxford University Press: Cambridge.

Chenery, H. B. (1960), 'Patterns of industrial growth', *American Economic Review*, 50(4), pp 534-654.

Chu, D. and G. W. K. Wong (1986), 'Foreign direct investment in China's Shenzhen Special Economic Zone: the strategies of firms from Hong Kong, Singapore, USA, and Japan', 3, *Issues in International Business*, pp.35-42.

Clark, C. (1957), *The Conditions of Economic Progress*, Macmillian: London.

Coase, R. H. 'The nature of the firm', *Economica*, 4, pp.386-405.

Cohen, K. S. and R. M. Cyert (1965), *Theory of the Firm: Resource Allocation in a Market Economy*, Prentice-Hall: Englewood Cliffs.

Conley, T. W. and P. W. Beamish, (1986), 'Joint ventures in China: legal implications', *Business Quarterly*, 51, pp.39-43.

Coughlin, C. C., J. Terza and V. Arromdee (1991), 'State characteristics and the location of foreign direct investment within the United States', *The Review of Economics and Statistics*, 73(4), pp.675-82.

Cromley, R. G. and M. B. Green (1985), 'Joint venture activity patterns of US firms, 1972-1979', *Growth and Change*, 16(3), pp.40-53.

Dahm, D. M. and M. B. Green (1995), 'Transnational branch banking 1976-1986: an empiricists's approach', in M. B. Green and R. McNaughton (eds.), *The Location of Foreign Direct Investment*, Avebury: Brookfield, pp.191-222.

Davidson, W. H. (1980), 'The location of foreign direct investment activity: country characteristics and experience effect', *Journal of International Business Studies*, 11(2), pp.9-22.

Dicken, P. (1971), 'Some aspects of the decision making behaviour of business organizations', *Economic Geography*, 47, pp.427-37.

Dicken, P. and P. Lloyd (1990), *Location in Space: Theoretical Perspectives in Economic Geography*, Harper and Row: New York.

Dicken, P. and P. Lloyd (1976), 'Geographical perspectives on United States investment in the United Kingdom', *Environment and Planning A*, 8, pp.685-705.

Dill, W. R. (1958), 'Environment as an influence on managerial autonomy', *Administrative Science Quarterly*, 2, pp.409-43.

Dorward, N. M. M. (1977), 'Market area analysis and product differentiation: a case study of the West German Truck Industry', in F. E. Hamilton and G. J. R. Linge (eds.) *Spatial Analysis, Industry, and the Industrial Environment, Vol. 1, Industrial Systems*, John Wiley: Chichester, pp.213-60.

Dunning, J. H. (1995), 'Reappraising the eclectic paradigm in an age of alliance capitalism', *Journal of International Business Studies*, 26(3), 461-91.

Dunning, J. H. (1993), *Multinational Enterprises and Global Economy*, Addison Wesley: New York.

Dunning, J. H. (1988a), 'The eclectic paradigm of international production: a restatement and some possible extensions', *Journal of International Business Studies*, 19(1), pp.1-31.

Dunning, J. H. (1988b), *Multinationals, Technology and Competitiveness*, Unwin Hyman: London.

Dunning, J. H. (1980), 'Towards an eclectic theory of international production: some empirical tests', *Journal of International Business Studies*, 11(1), pp.9-31.

Dunning, J. H. (1979), 'Explaining changing patterns of international production: in defence of the eclectic theory', *Oxford Bulletin of Economies and Statistics*, 41, pp.269-96.

Dunning, J. H. (1973), 'The determinants of international production', *Oxford Economic Papers*, 25(3), pp.289-336.

Dunning, J. H. (1958), *American Investment in British Manufacturing*, Allen and Unwin: London.

Edgington, D. W. (1995), 'Japanese manufacturing companies in southern Ontario and NAFTA', in M. B. Green and R. McNaughton (eds.) *The Location of Foreign Direct Investment*, Avebury: Brookfield, USA, pp.85-104.

Emery, F. E. and E. L. Trist, (1965), 'The causal texture of organizational environments', *Human Relations*, 18, pp.21-31.

Gandhi, P. (1986), 'Foreign direct investment and regional development: the case of Canadian investment in New York State', in M. Schoolman and A. Magid (eds.) *Reindustrializing New York State: Strategies, Implications and Challenges*, State University of New York Press: Albany, pp.205-27.

Gerig, T. (1994), *Competition Markets*, Working Paper: 55, Center for Economic Policy Research, University of Basel, Switzerland.

Ghoshal, S. and C. A. Bartlett (1990), 'The multinational corporations as an interorganizational network', *Academy of Management Review*, 15(4), pp.603-25.

Gilmour, J. M. (1974), 'External economies of scale, internal industrial linkages and decision making in manufacturing', in F. E. Hamilton (ed.) *Spatial Perspectives on Industrial Organization and Decision-making*, John Wiley and Sons: London, pp.335-62.

Glickman, N.J. and D. Woodward (1988), 'The location of foreign direct investment in the United States: patterns and determinants', *International Regional Science Review*, 11(2), pp.137-54.

Goddard, J. (1975), *Office Location in Urban and Regional Development*, London: Oxford University Press.

Gray, H.P. (1972), *The Economics of Business Investment Abroad*, Macmillian: New York.

Goodnow, J.D. and J. E. Hansz (1972), 'Environmental determinants of overseas market entry strategies', *Journal of International Business Studies*, 3(1), pp.33-50.

Green, M. B. (1987), 'Corporate-merger-defined core-peripheral relations for the United States', *Growth and Change*, 18(3), pp.12-35.

Green, M. B. (1985), 'Canadian corporate joint venture activity, 1971-1981: aggregate patterns', *Urban Geography*, 6(4), pp.352-69.

Green, M. B. and R. G. Cromley (1986), 'United States: foreign joint venture patterns', *Tijdschrift voor Econ. En Soc. Geografie*, 77(2), pp.103-112.

Green, M. B. and R. G. Cromley (1982), 'The horizontal merger: its motives and spatial employment impacts', *Economic Geography*, 59, pp.358-69.

Grubaugh, S.G. (1987a), 'The process of direct foreign investment', *Southern Economic Journal*, 54(2), pp.351-58.

Grubaugh, S.G. (1987b), 'Determinants of direct foreign investment', *The Review of Economics and Statistics*, 69(1), pp.149-52.

Haigh, R. W. (1989), *Investment Strategies and the Plant-Location Decision: Foreign Companies in the United States*, Praeger:New York.

Hakanson, L. (1977), 'Towards a theory of location and corporate growth', in F. E. Hamilton and G. J. R. Linge (eds.) *Spatial Analysis, Industry, and the Industrial Environment, Vol.1, Industrial Systems*, John Wiley: Chichester, pp.115-38.

Hamilton, F. E. (1974), 'A view of spatial behavior, industrial organizations and decision making', in F. E. Hamilton (ed.) *Spatial Perspectives on Industrial Organization and Decision-making*, John Wiley and Sons: London, pp.3-46.

Hayter, R. and H. D. Watts (1983), 'The geography of enterprise: a reappraisal', *Progress in Human Geography*, 7(2), pp.157-81.

Hill, S. and M. Munday (1992), 'The UK regional distribution of foreign direct investment : analysis and determinants', *Regional Studies*, 25(6), pp.535-44.

Hirsch, S. (1976), 'An international trade and investment theory of the firm', *Oxford Economic Papers*, 28(2), pp.258-70.

Hirschman, A. O. (1958), *The Strategy of Economic Development*, Yale University Press: New Haven.

Hoffmann, W.G. (1958), *The Growth of Industrial Economies*, Manchester University Press: Manchester.

Hofstede, G. (1983), 'The cultural relativity of organizational practices and theories,' *Journal of International Business Studies*, 14(3), pp.75-89.

Horst, T. O.(1972b), 'Firm and industry determinants of the decision to invest abroad: an empirical study', *The Review of Economics and Statistics*, 54(3), pp. 258-66.

Horst, T.O. (1974), 'The theory of the firm', in J. H. Dunning (ed.), *Economic Analysis and Multinational Enterprise*, George Allen and Unwin: London, pp.31-46.

Hotelling, H. (1929), 'Stability in competition', *Economic Journal*, 39, pp.41-57.

Hymer, S. H. (1976), *The International Operations of National Firms: A Study of Direct Foreign Investment*, MIT Press: Cambridge, MA.

International Monetary Fund (1985), *Foreign Direct Investment in Developing Countries*, IMF: Washington, DC.

Kindleberger, C.P. (1969), *American Business Abroad: Six Lectures on Direct Investment*, Yale University Press: New Haven.

Knickerbocker, F. T. (1973), *Oligopolistic Reaction and Multinational Enterprises*, Harvard University Press: Cambridge, MA.

Koechlin, T. (1992), 'The determinants of the location of USA direct foreign investment', *International Review of Applied Economics*, 6(2), pp.203-16.

Kogut, B. (1988), 'Joint ventures: theoretical and empirical perspectives', *Strategic Management Journal*, 9(4), pp.31-32.

Kogut, B. and H. Singh (1988), 'The effect of national culture on the choice of entry mode', *Journal of International Business Studies*, 19(3), pp.411-32.

Kojima, K. (1982), 'Macroeconomic versus international business approach to direct foreign investment', *Hitotsubashi Journal of Economics*, 23, pp.1-19.

Korbin, S. J. (1976), 'The environmental determinants of foreign direct manufacturing investment: an ex post empirical analysis', *Journal of International Business Studies*, 7(2), pp.29-42.

Kravis, I. B. and R. E. Lipsey (1982), 'The location ,of overseas production for export by US multinational firms', *Journal of International Economics*, 12, pp.201-23.

Lall, S. (1978a), 'Transnationals, domestic enterprises, and industrial structure in host LDCs: a survey', *Oxford Economic Papers*, 30(3), pp.215-48.

Lall, S. (1978b), 'The pattern of intra-firm exports by US multinationals', *Oxford Bulletin of Economics and Statistics*, 3(40), pp.209-22.

Lall, S. (1979), 'The international allocation of research activity by US multinationals', *Oxford Bulletin of Economics and Statistics*, 41(4), pp.313-30.

Lall, S. (1980), 'Monopolistic advantages and foreign involvement by US manufacturing industry', *Oxford Economic Papers*, 32(1), pp.102-122.

Lall, S. (1983), *The New Multinationals: the Spread of Third World Enterprises*, John Wiley and Sons: New York.

Lauger, M. I. and S. Shetty (1985), 'Determinants of foreign plant start-ups in the United States: lessons for policy-makers in the Southeast', *Vanderbilt Journal of Transnational Law*, 19, pp.223-45.

Law, C. M. (1980), 'The foreign company's location investment decision and its role in British regional development', *Tijdschrift voor Econ. en Soc. Geografie*, 71(1), pp.15-20.

Lecraw, D. (1977), 'Direct investment by firms from less developed countries', *Oxford Economic Papers*, 29(3), pp.442-57.

Leung, C. K. (1990), 'Locational characteristics of foreign equity joint venture investment in China: 1979-1985', *Professional Geographer*, 42(4), pp.403-21.

Lever, W. (1974), 'Manufacturing linkages and the search for suppliers and markets', in F. E. Hamilton (ed.) *Spatial Perspectives on Industrial Organization and Decision-making*, John Wiley and Sons: London, pp.309-34.

Lewis, W. A. (1958), 'Economic development with unlimited supplies of labour', in A. N. Agarwala and S. P. Singh (eds.) *The Economics of Underdevelopment*, Oxford University Press: London, pp.400-49.

Lim, D. (1983), 'Fiscal incentives and direct foreign investment in less developed countries', *The Journal of Development Studies*, 19(2), pp.207-12.

Liu, H. and M. Fujita (1991), 'A monopolistic competition model of spatial agglomeration with variable density', *Annals of Regional Science*, 25(2), pp.81-99.

Lloyd, P. E. and P. Dicken (1977), *Location in Space: A Theoretical Approach to Economic Geography,* Harper and Row: London.

MacMillan, K. and D. Farmer (1978), 'Redefining the boundaries of the firm', *The Journal of Industrial Economics*, 27, pp.277-86.

McConnell, J. E. (1980), 'Foreign direct investment in the United States', *Annals of the Association of American Geographers*, 70(2), pp.259-70.

McConnell, J. E. (1983), 'The international location of manufacturing investment: recent behaviour of foreign-owned corporations in the United States', in F. E. Hamilton and G. J. R. Linge, (eds.) *Spatial Analysis, Industry, and the Industrial Environments Vol. 3*, John Wiley: Chichester, pp.337-58.

McDermott, P. J. (1977), 'Overseas investment and the industrial geography of the United Kingdom', *Area,* 9(3), pp.200-7.

McDermott, P. and M. Taylor (1982), *Industrial Organization and Location,* Cambridge University Press: Cambridge.

McNee, R. (1974), 'A systems approach to understanding the geographic behavior of organizations, especially large corporations', in F. E. Hamilton (ed.) *Spatial Perspectives on Industrial Organization and Decision-making*, John Wiley and Sons: London, pp.47-76.

Malecki, E. J. (1980), 'Corporate organization of R and D and the location of technological activities', *Regional Studies*, 14, pp.219-34.

Mamanie, D. (1994), 'The scope for pure profits in a standard location model', *Journal of Regional Science*, 34(1), pp.27-38.

Massey, D. (1978), 'Capital and locational change: the UK electrical engineering and electronic industry', *Review of Radical Political Economics*, 10, pp.39-54.

Massey, D. (1979), 'A critical evaluation of industrial location theory', in F. E. Hamilton, and G. J. R. Linge (eds.) *Spatial Analysis, Industry, and the Industrial Environment, Vol.1, Industrial Systems*, John Wiley: Chichester, pp.57-72.

Massey, D. and R. A. Meegan, (1979), 'The geography of industrial reorganization: the spatial effects of restructuring of the electrical engineering sector under the industrial reorganization corporation', *Progress in Planning*, 10, pp.155-237.

Meyer, S. and T. Qu (1995), 'Place-specific determinants of FDI: the geographical perspective', in M. B. Green and R. B. McNaughton (eds.), *The Location of Foreign Direct Investment*, Avebury: Brookfield, USA, pp.1-13.

Moore, M. L., B. M. Steece, and C. W. Swenson (1987), 'An analysis of the impact of state income rates and bases on foreign investment', *Accounting Review*, 62, pp.671-85.

Moxon, R. W. (1975), 'The motivation for investment in offshore plants: the case of the US electronics industry', *Journal of International Business Studies*, 6(1), pp.51-66.

North, D. (1974), 'The process of locational change in different manufacturing organizations', in F. E. Hamilton (ed.) *Spatial Perspectives on Industrial Organization and Decision-making*, John Wiley and Sons: London, pp.213-45.

Ó hUallacháin, B. (1984a), 'Input-output linkages and foreign investment in Ireland', *International Regional Science Review*, 9(3), pp.185-200.

Ó hUallacháin, B. (1984b), 'Linkages and foreign investment in the United States', *Economic Geography*, 60, pp.238-53.

Ó hUallacháin, B. (1985a), 'The role of foreign direct investment in the development of regional industrial systems: current knowledge and suggestions for a future American research agenda', *Regional Studies*, 20(2), pp.151-62.

Ó hUallacháin, B. (1985b), 'Spatial patterns of foreign direct investment in the United States', *Professional Geographer*, 37(2), pp.155-63.

Ondrich, J. and M. Wasylenko (1993), *Foreign direct investment in the United States*, Kalamazoo, Michigan: W. E. Upjohn Institute for Employment Research.

Ozawa, T. (1979), 'International investment and industrial structure: new theoretical implications from the Japanese experience', *Oxford Economic Papers*, 31(1), pp.72-92.

Penrose, E. T. (1959), *The theory of the growth of the firm*, Basil Blackwell, Oxford.

Poniachek, H. A. (1986), *Direct foreign investment in the United States*, Lexington Books, New York.

Porter, M. (1991), 'Towards a dynamic theory of strategy', *Strategic Management Journal*, 12, pp.95-117.

Porter, M. (1990), *The Competitive Advantage of Nations*, The Free Press: New York.

Porter, M.(1986), *Competition in Global Industries*, Harvard Business School Press: Boston.

Pred, A. (1967), *Behavior and Location, Part I*, Lund Studies in Geography, Series B: Human Geography, No. 27, Gleerup: Lund.

Pred, A. (1969), *Behavior and Location, Part II*, Lund Studies in Geography, Series B: Human Geography, No. 28, Gleerup: Lund.

Pred, A. (1974), 'Industry, information and city-system interdependencies', in F. E. Hamilton (ed.) *Spatial Perspectives on Industrial Organization and Decision-making*, John Wiley and Sons: London, pp.105-42.

Rees, J. (1978b), 'On the spatial spread and oligopolistic behaviour of large rubber companies', *Geoform*, 9, pp.319-30.

Rees, J. (1974), 'Decision-making, the growth of the firm and the business environment', in F. E. Hamilton (ed.) *Spatial Perspectives on Industrial Organization and Decision-making*, John Wiley and Sons: London, pp.189-212.

Rees, J. (1978a), 'Manufacturing headquarters in a postindustrial context', *Economic Geography*, 54, pp.337-54.

Reuber, G. L. (1973), *Private Foreign Investment in Development*, Clarendon Press: Oxford.

Richardson, H. W. (1969), *Regional Economics: Location Theory, Urban Structure and Change*, Praeger: New York.

Riedel, J. (1976), 'The nature and determinants of export-oriented direct foreign investment in a developing country: a case study of Taiwan', *Weltwirschaftliche Archiv.*, 111(3), pp.505-26.

Rolfe, R. J., D. A. Ricks, M. M. Pointer, and M. McCarthy (1993), 'Determinants of FDI incentive preferences of MNEs', *Journal of International Business Studies*, 23(2), pp.335-55.

Root, F. R. and A. A. Ahmed (1979), 'Empirical determinants of manufacturing foreign investment in developing countries', *Economic Development and Cultural Change*, 27(4), pp.751-67.

Rostow, W. W. (1956), 'The take-off into self-sustained growth' in A. N. Agarwala and S. P. Singh (eds.) *The Economics of Underdevelopment*, Oxford University Press: London, pp.154-88.

Rostow, W. W. (1960), *The Stages of Economic Growth: A Non-Communist Manifesto,* MIT Press, Cambridge.

Roth, K. and A. J. Morrision (1992), 'Implementing global strategy: characteristics of global subsidiary mandates', *Journal of International Business Studies*, 23(4), pp.715-36.

Ruggles, R. L. Jr. (1983), 'The environment for American business ventures in the People's Republic of China', *Columbia Journal of World Business*, 18(4), pp.67-73.

Rugman, A.M., D. J. Lecraw, and L. D. Booth (1985), *International Business: Firm and Environment*, McGraw-Hill: New York.

Scaperlanda A. E. and L. J. Mauer (1969), 'The determinants of US direct investment in the EEC', *American Economic Review*, 59, pp.558-68.

Schive, C. and K. T. Hsueh (1985), *Taiwan's Investment in ASEAN Countries and its Competitiveness*, ROC National University: Taipei.

Schive, C. (1990), 'Direct foreign investment and linkage effects: the experience of Taiwan', *Canadian Journal of Development Studies*, 11(2), pp.325-42.

Schneider, F. and B. S. Frey (1985), 'Economic and political determinants of foreign direct investment', *World Development*, 13(2), pp.161-75.

Scholer, K. (1993), 'Consistent conjectural variations in a two-dimensional spatial market', *Regional Science and Urban Economics*, 23(6), pp.765-88.

Schroath, F. W., M. Y. Hu, and H. Cen (1993), 'Country of origin effects of foreign investment in the People's Republic of China', *Journal of International Business*, pp.277-90.

Shan, W. (1991), 'Environmental risks and joint venture sharing agreements', *Journal of International Business Studies*, 22(4), pp.555-78.

Shan, W. (1989), 'Reform of China's foreign trade system: experiences and prospects', *China Economic Review*, Spring, pp.33-35.

Smith, D. M. (1981), *Industrial Geography: An Economic Geographical Analysis*, 2nd ed., John Wiley: New York.

Stafford, H. A. (1974), 'The anatomy of the location decision : content analysis of case studies', in F. E. Hamilton (ed.) *Spatial Perspectives on Industrial Organization and Decision-making*, John Wiley and Sons: London, pp.169-88.

Steed, G. P. F. (1971), 'Plant adaption, firm environments and locational analysis' *Professional Geographer*, 23(4), pp.324-27.

Stobaugh, R. B. Jr. (1969), 'How to analyse foreign investment climate', *Harvard Business Review*, 47, pp.100-108.

Storper, M. (1981), 'Toward a structural theory of industria location', in Rees, J., G. J. D. Hewings and H. A. Stafford (eds.) *Industrial Location and Regional Systems*, Croom Helm: London, pp.17-40.

Storper, M. and R. Walker (1983), 'The theory of labour and the theory of location', *International Journal of Urban and Regional Research*, 7(1), pp.1-43.

Stuckey, J. A. (1983), *Vertical integration and joint ventures in the aluminum industry*, Harvard University Press: Cambridge, MA.

Tao, J. (1988), 'Cooperative joint ventures in China', *International Financial Law Review*, 7(10), pp.34-36.

Taylor, M. J. (1975), 'Organizational growth, spatial interaction, and locational decision-making', *Regional Studies*, 9, pp.313-23.

Taylor, M. J. and N. J. Thrift (1982), 'Models of corporate development and the multinational corporation', in M. J. Taylor and N. J. Thrift (eds.) *The Geography of Multinationals*, Croom Helm: London , pp.14-32.

Thompson, J. D. (1967), *Organizations in Action*, New York: McGraw-Hill.

Tong, H. (1979), *Plant Location Decisions of Foreign Manufacturing Investors*, UMI Research Press, Ann Arbor, MI.

Townroe, P.M. (1974), 'Post-move stability and the location decision', in F. E. Hamilton (ed.) *Spatial Perspectives on Industrial Organization and Decision-making*, London: John Wiley and Sons, pp.287-308.

US-China Business Council (1988), *Special report on US investment in China*, The China Business Forum: Washington, DC.

Vernon, R. (1966), 'International investment and international trade in the product cycle', *Quarterly Journal of Economics*, 80, May.

Vernon, R. (1971), *Sovereignty at Bay: the Multinational Spread of US Enterprises*, Basic Books: New York .

Vernon, R. (1974), 'The location of economic activity', in J. H. Dunning (ed.), *Economic Analysis and Multinational Enterprise*, Allen and Unwin: London, pp.89-114.

Vernon, R. (1979), 'The product cycle hypothesis in a new international environment', *Oxford Bulletin of Economics and Statistics*, 41(4), pp.255-67.

Walker, R. (1988), 'The geographical organization of production-systems', *Environment and Planning D*, 6(4), pp.377-408.

Walker, R. and M. Storper (1981), 'Capital and industrial location', *Progress in Human Geography*, 5(4), pp.473-509.

Watts, H. D. (1987), *Industrial Geography*, John Wiley and Sons: New York.

Watts, H. D. (1980a), *The Large Industrial Enterprise: Some Spatial Perspectives*, Croom Helm: London.

Watts, H. D. (1980b), 'The location of European direct investment in the United Kingdom', *Tijdschrift voor Econ. en Soc. Geografie*, 71(1), pp.3-14.

Watts, H. D. (1979), 'Large firms, multinationals, and regional development: some new evidence from the United Kingdom', *Environment and Planning A*, 11, pp.71-81.

Weber, A. (1929), *Alfred Weber's Theory of the Location of Industries*, University of Chicago Press: Chicago.

Wells, L. T. (1983), *Third World Multinationals*, the MIT Press: Cambridge, MA.

Wells. L. T. (1977), 'The internationalization of firms from developing countries', in T. Agmon and C. P. Kindleberger (eds.), *Multinationals from Small Countries*, MIT Press: Cambridge, MA., pp.133-56.

Wells, L. T. (1972) (ed.) *The Product Cycle and International Trade*, Harvard University Press: Cambridge, MA.

White, R. E. and T. A. Poynter (1984), 'Strategies for foreign-owned subsidaries in Canada', *Business Quarterly*, 49, pp.59-69.

Woodward, D. P. (1992), 'Locational determinants of Japanese manufacturing start-ups in the United States', *Southern Economic Journal*, 58(3), pp, 690-708.

Xie, Y. and A. K. Dutt (1993), 'Foreign joint ventures in the People's Republic of China, 1979-85', *GeoJournal*, 29(4), pp.385-97.

Xie, Y. and F. J. Costa (1991), 'The impact of economic reforms on the urban economy of The People's Republic of China', *Professional Geographer*, 43(3), pp.318-35.

Yannopolous, G. N. and J. H. Dunning (1976), 'Multi-national enterprise and regional development: an exploratory paper', *Regional Studies*, 10, pp.389-401.

Yeon, Y. D. (1992), 'The determinants of Korean foreign direct investment in manufacturing industries', *Weltwirtschftliches Archiv*, 128(3), pp.527-41.

Yu, C. M. J. (1990), 'The experience effect and foreign direct investment', *Weltsirtshaftliche Archiv*, 126, pp.561-80.

Laws and Regulations of People's Republic China and Official Reports Citied:

The Patent Law of the People's Republic of China, adopted on March 12, 1984 at the Fourth Session of the Standing Committee of the Sixth National People's Congress.

The Law of the People's Republic of China on Joint Ventures Using Chinese and Foreign Investment, adopted on July 1, 1979 and promulgated on July 8, 1979.

Regulations for the Implementation of the Law on Joint Ventures Using Chinese and Foreign Investment, promulgated by the State Council on September 20, 1983

Xinhua News Agency (July 12, 1984), *On the special polices concerning the opening of the fourteen coastal open cities by the relevant Director from the State Council.*

'The law of the People's Republic of China on wholly foreign owned enterprises, April 14, 1986', *the Almanac*, 1987, pp.94-95 (in Chinese),

'The law of the People's Republic of China on Sino-foreign cooperative joint ventures, April 3, 1988', *the Almanac*, 1989, pp.102-103 (in Chinese),

'Provisions of the State Council on the foreign exchange balancing in Sino-foreign joint ventures', issued by the State Council on January 15, 1986, in *the Almanac*, 1987, pp.93-94 (in Chinese),

'Excerpt of the Sixth Five Year (1981-1985) Plan of social and economic development of PR China', in *the Almanac of China's Foreign Economic Relations and Trade*, 1983, Hong Kong: China Resources Advertising Co. Ltd., pp.11-13.

'Excerpt of the Sixth Five Year Plan of Social and economic development of People's Republic of China (1986-90)', in *the Almanac of China's Foreign Economic Relations and Trade*, 1987, Hong Kong: China Resources Advertising Co. Ltd..

'Excerpt of suggestions from the Central Committee of Chinese Communist Party concerning the Seventh Five Year plan of social and economic development', in *the Almanac of China's Foreign Economic Relations and Trade*, 1986, Hong Kong: China Resources Advertising Co. Ltd., pp.3-11.

'The great success in the importation of technology in 1985', in *the Almanac*, 1986, pp.41-43 (in Chinese)

'A brief account on the importation of technology in 1988', in *the Almanac*, 1989, pp.49-50, (in Chinese)

'Provisions of the State Council of the People's Republic of China for the encouragement of foreign investment', promulgated by the State Council on October 11, 1986, in *the Almanac*, 1987, pp.96-98 (in Chinese),

'Implementing procedures on the certification of export ventures and advanced technology ventures, promoted by the Ministry of Foreign Economic Relations and Trade (MOFERT) on January 27, 1987', in *the Almanac*, 1988, pp.110-111 (in Chinese),

'Zhao Ziyang on the strategies for economic development in coastal regions', in *the Almanac*, 1988, pp.27-32 (in Chinese),

'Excerpt of the government work report', in *the Almanac*, 1989, pp.1-9 (in Chinese),

'Excerpt of Vice Premier Tian Jiyun's address to the working conference on the opening of coastal regions', in *the Almanac*, pp.15-9 (in Chinese),

'Excerpt of Comrade Gu Mu's Address to the working conference on the opening of coastal regions', in *the Almanac*, 1989, pp.25, 32 (in Chinese),

194

Circular of the State Council on the Ratification of the establishment of national high and technology development zones and related policy and regulations', in *the Almanac*, 1992 (in Chinese),

'Criteria for and identification of high and new technology ventures in national high and new technology development zones, State Science and Technology Commission', in *the Almanac*, 1992, (in Chinese),

'Some Temporary policy concerning national high and new technological industry development zones, State Science and Technology Commission', in *the Almanac*, 1992, (in Chinese),

'Tax policy concerning national high and new technological industry development zones, state taxation bureau, adopted in March 1991', in *the Almanac*, 1992, (in Chinese)

For Product Safety Concerns and Information please contact our EU
representative GPSR@taylorandfrancis.com Taylor & Francis Verlag GmbH,
Kaufingerstraße 24, 80331 München, Germany

Printed and bound by CPI Group (UK) Ltd, Croydon, CR0 4YY
08/05/2025
01864370-0005